MEDICINAL COOKERY
DALE PINNOCK

MEDICINAL COOKERY

DALE PINNOCK

Recipes from nature's edible pharmacy

CONTENTS

NATURE'S EDIBLE PHARMACY   173

An A-Z guide to the most powerful common medicinal foods on the planet in the following categories:

A NEW PARADIGM IN FOOD

Our attitudes to food aren't what they used to be. There once was a time when we Brits consumed some of the dullest food in history. Our staple cuisine seemed something of a joke to the rest of the world. Over-boiled vegetables and soggy mashed potatoes were the order of the day. During the last decade or so, however, we have had a food revolution. We have become a nation that, finally, is becoming better educated when it comes to the food that we eat.

We are becoming far more conscious of our choices and more discerning when it comes to the quality of the food that we eat. Food heroes such as Jamie Oliver and Hugh Fearnley-Whittingstall have shown us all that is good – and all that is incredibly bad – about the food industry. With that know-ledge has also come an increased awareness of the fact that the food we eat doesn't move through our bodies without affecting us. We have finally understood that what we eat will have an impact on our health.

Demand for healthy options and infor-mation on healthy eating has skyrocketed. Granted, with that come all manner of weird claims and peculiar diets, but finally the realisation is there. We are at a point where research abounds that shows that our diet is one of the most powerful and relevant elements of 'self-healthcare'. We know more than ever about the way in which our dietary patterns may make us more susceptible to disease, offer profound protection against the common killers and most excitingly, in my opinion, actively work as a therapeutic intervention. That's my main focus.

I have to say right from the get go that I have zero interest in being an 'alternative' to, or to represent something that is against, drug treatments. I am not in any way, shape or form of that persuasion. My personal stance is that healthcare isn't a single science or art. It has many facets. If you have serious health issues which require drugs, then you require drugs! No question. No argument. I take enormous issue with those who flagrantly parade a specific diet as the next all-encompassing panacea. My stance is that nutrition is a very powerful and effective therapeutic intervention as part of the healthcare picture. It is the one part that we can actively engage in. It doesn't matter what issue you are facing. Whether it's something life-threatening or a swollen thumb – the food you eat and the lifestyle you lead will have an impact on it.

Food – or rather the nutrients within food – interact directly with, and influence, our physiology. So, our diet and lifestyle represents an area of healthcare that we can actively get involved in. We aren't powerless and idle in our healthcare. This stance has led me to work with hundreds of GPs and academics. During my postgraduate studies, many of my fellow students on the Nutritional Medicine MSc at the University of Surrey were GPs or medics of some kind. I aim in my work to be a bridge between science and the media – a voice of sense and sanity amid the din.

MY STORY

When I was ten, I started to change. I noticed a few little bumps on my chin. Being a child, I wasn't overly concerned, as there were far more important things to worry about – fishing was my distraction of choice back then. The only thing that mattered was getting down to the lake after school and at the weekends.

A year later, it was time to wave goodbye to junior school and head off to secondary school (high school). It was here that the trouble began. By this stage I was spotty. There's no other word for it. From forehead to chin, I was covered in nasty little red spots. It didn't take long for everyone else in the class to notice this too. As you can guess, kids being the way they are, the usual names came: Pizzaface, Zitface, and so on. At that stage in life, these things can make us very self-conscious and I became quite withdrawn, although I'd never let it show. By the time I reached the final year of school, it was a permanent distraction. I went to doctor after doctor, specialist after specialist, and tried every conceivable lotion and potion they had to offer. Strange sticky roll-on lotions, antibiotics, retinol gels – the works. Nothing whatsoever helped.

One day, when I was about fifteen or sixteen, a friend's mum lent me a book on nutrition and natural healthcare. I remember her telling me, 'Unless you look after what's going on inside, nothing will change on the outside.' Now, as a teenage boy, you can imagine the sceptical expletives that spouted forth. However, I was desperate beyond all measure (I hated even being seen in daylight), so I read the book. I read it from cover to cover in a weekend, and changed my lifestyle immediately as a result. I gave up smoking and most dairy products and built a diet based on fruits, vegetables and wholegrains. I supplemented it with things like zinc, omega 3 and the B vitamins.

The changes were incredible. My skin certainly did clear. The red aggressive acne eventually disappeared, leaving not even the slightest mark. Beyond that, I rebuilt my body and mind from the ground up, and an entirely new person was born. I have seen the powerful effect that food can have on our health, first hand. It is simple yet profound. It was this experience that led me here today.

IMPORTANT SAFETY NOTE

If you are concerned about any aspect of your health, or wish to change your diet to address your concerns, you must consult your doctor. The information in this book should not be treated as a substitute for medical advice.

FOOD AND MEDICINE
NO SEPARATION

OK, so Hippocrates' famous quote, 'Let food be thy medicine, and thy medicine by thy food' has been used more times than I care to think about. But the fact that it has gone down in history without question is testament to its relevance. Every recorded healing system on the planet, through every historical age, has recognised the vitally important role that food has to play, both in maintaining good health and in treating disease. Many ancient cultures relied almost entirely on food remedies as their source of medicine, and many, such as Ayurveda, Traditional Chinese Medicine and Egyptian medicine, studied the intricate relationships between food and physiological functions for millennia. Often, they used terms that relate to supposed 'energetic' patterns and activities in foods, and how these interplay with similar energetic patterns and events in the body, to cause either balance or harm. These were not irrelevant observations at

all, it's more the case that such observations were described and documented in accordance with the cultural and scientific paradigms that existed at the time. In that culture and historical period, they were very relevant. Oddly enough, many such observations can essentially be explained by our modern understanding of the subject. Same thing, different semantics.

In the last two centuries, the study of the relationship between food, our bodies and our health has been moving at a fast pace. Quite early on, we discovered things such as proteins and carbohydrates, fats and the most obvious macroelements of the nutritional picture, realising their importance in energy production, building our bodies and tissue maintenance. Piece by piece, we became aware of the individual vitamins and the physiological roles that they play. We became all too aware of the negative consequences of being deficient in these vital compounds, resulting in diseases such as scurvy, rickets and beriberi, but research seldom concentrated on the potential of these compounds to actively heal the body. At that point we were focused on what might happen if we didn't consume enough of them. We hadn't begun to understand that their presence may actually promote good health and influence our physiology in such a way that they may be a treatment in their own right.

As nutritional science progressed, focus moved to things such as the calorie, saturated and unsaturated fats, and body mass index (BMI). These are many of the elements of what I call nutritional physiology that we understand inside out (although if you want a work of fiction, many calorie and saturated fat stories are full enough of fantasy to make the mind boggle). But the next stage, the point at which nutrition can actively play a positive and relevant role in human health-care, is a new science. That's not to say that it is an immature science, but more the case that interest in it and understanding of how to conduct this science is new. But thankfully the science is motoring forward at a fast pace.

We know with absolute certainty that nutrition alone has more than just a simple maintenance role – much much more. So many of us for so long just thought that eating was simply an exercise in refuelling! Simply eat a good hearty meal to fill you up and get you through until the next meal. Now we know very differently. The macro-nutrients – proteins, fats and carbohydrates – are the energy, repair and structural nutrients. The micronutrients – vitamins, minerals and trace elements – however, go way beyond this. They are in essence biochemical facilitators within the body. This means that they directly influence the activity of very specific and vital physiological events, metabolic pathways and biochemical reactions within our bodies. They basically make stuff happen. They either directly make things happen, help manufacture the things that make things happen or assist the things that make things happen! Without the right amounts of them we are in trouble.

To this end, a few smart individuals began to realise that the manipulation of nutrient intake and the tweaking and tailoring of our diet can have a huge impact upon both the severity and the progression of disease. This is because it can directly affect the internal biochemical terrain. In doing so it supports the mechanisms that abound in the body which allow this wonderful machine to repair and regulate itself. I really don't like the word healing as it has become far too hippy-dippy now, but in essence that is what the body can do for itself, providing it is given an environment conducive to that.

Let's use the example of a cut on your finger. After a few minutes, the bleeding stops. Within a few hours, a scab has formed, and the body is well under way with repairing the damaged tissue. Now, if we were to continually pick at the scab, it would cause the wound to bleed and prevent healing from taking place. Well, eating a diet that consists of processed food, full of refined junk and devoid of nutrients, is the equivalent of picking at that scab. But if we consume a diet of fresh, wholesome, unadulterated ingredients, we are, in fact, creating an environment that is conducive to healing.

To illustrate the above, let's look at dietary fats. Whatever you may believe or have read in the past, fats – the right ones – are a vital part of the human diet. They can have a massive impact upon both the onset of disease and the body's ability to manage it. When we metabolise (chemically process, following digestion and absorption) certain fats, our body produces a whole range of by-products, from structural materials that maintain cells, through to compounds that regulate some quite complex chemical reactions. One such group is a series of biochemical messengers called prostaglandins. These complex molecules, among other things, are involved in either the instigation and enhancement, or the prevention and reduction, of pain and inflammation, depending on which type is produced. This can be greatly influenced by the type of dietary fats we consume. If we eat predominantly fats that fall into the omega 3 polyunsaturated fat category, then we will direct our bodies to make a far higher percentage of the type of prostaglandins that help to reduce inflammation and minimise pain. However, if we eat more fats from the omega 6 family, then we direct our bodies to manufacture more of the prostaglandins that instigate and enhance pain and inflammation. It is obvious that increasing inflammation can worsen and even trigger certain conditions and complications. Many of the chronic diseases that are causing problems in the modern world have inflammation at their root. Cardiovascular disease, for example, is triggered by inflammation within the vessel walls. Chronic inflammation in tissues can trigger cellular changes that can lead to tumour formation. So reducing inflammation can have a significant impact on our long-term health, and something as simple as changing the types of fats that we consume can have a massive impact upon this.

This is a minuscule glance at the influence that dietary changes can have on our internal environment in a way that can help to manage disease. For this reason, I personally feel that there is no separation between food and medicine. If applied in the right way under the right guidance, the results can be equally powerful.

All of the above refers to the study of nutrition; what we know about the way in which nutrients actually interact with our bodies and the healing potential that nutrition offers. However, the staggering results that we observe when people change their diets to only include minimally processed foods, far exceed the physical changes that we would expect to see from merely increasing our nutritional profile. There are other elements present in these foods that act as incredibly powerful medicines. This hidden magic is revealed in the next chapter.

PHYTOCHEMICALS
THE PHARMACY IN OUR FOOD

PHYTO = PLANT.

As is now becoming clear, food has the ability to drastically harm or profoundly heal. Simple changes in diet can have gargantuan influences upon our physiology. Skin conditions, inflammatory diseases, digestive ailments, low immunity – these can all be influenced in varying degrees by dietary interventions.

At last there is a huge body of research coming to the forefront and from that a great deal of scientific investigation has focused upon nutrition as a healing modality in its own right. The role of every conceivable nutrient has now been studied in the context of disease prevention and management. We are aware of the way in which every nutrient interacts with metabolic functions and biochemical pathways in a way that can influence specific biochemical outcomes. We know the clinical implications of

low levels of certain nutrients, and we have theorised about the many ways in which to address this in the clinical setting. However, it seems that focusing on purely the nutritional element of food always seems to fall short. The use of nutritional supplements never delivers the same level of healing and transformation as occurs when a complete dietary overhaul is undertaken. I do take supplements and believe that they have their place, but bundled nutrients or individual nutrients cannot replicate the complexity of a wholefood. There is simply more going on in wholefoods. Nutrition is just one part of an incredibly broad, complex and wondrous picture. Fresh plant foods, in particular, contain a whole cocktail of substances that reach so far beyond the scope of nutrition alone. These substances are the phytochemicals.

The realisation that I came to at different stages of my career led me to unlock the secrets that food hold. The initial stages of this began in the late 1990s. I began experimenting with my health as a teenager. I tried every supplement, exercise programme and diet you could imagine. The only thing that ever really caused a huge shift in my health was a diet focused around wholefoods. Whenever I went back to a diet that was more like the typical Western diet, but accompanied by a whole cocktail of nutritional supplements, I would start feeling awful and the benefits I had once experienced began to decline. From the nutritional perspective, I was taking in a level of nutrients that should, according to all the supplement gurus, leave me feeling super-human. But no! Something was missing, and I knew it was more than nutrition alone. During my nutrition studies, I thought I might find the answer, but sadly didn't. We spoke about weird arbitrary terms such as BMI (which I have renamed Banal, Meaningless, Irrelevant), and measuring calories and fat. It wasn't until I began my degree in Herbal Medicine at London's University of Westminster that the penny finally dropped, and I suddenly made sense of what fresh food was delivering that supplements did not.

Now I'm not going to lie, some of the science was questionable. But I started the course not to be a herbalist, but to learn about the science of phytochemistry, which was taught by the School of Biosciences, so it was strong in its content (as were the pathology, differential diagnosis, pharmacology and clinical skills elements of the course, which all added to my understanding). Phytochemistry is plant biochemistry. The course I was on was basically *applied* phytochemistry: how plant biochemistry interacts with human physiological systems in order to bring about changes that one could say are conducive to healing and correct functioning again. I learnt that pharmacologists and pharmacognosists (people who study the medicinal chemistry of plants) had unlocked the biochemical secrets that made the healing plants of ancient texts clearly valid in the modern scientific world. It was at that point the connection between the biochemistry of plants and healing dawned on me. I knew that there were many very dull and dry texts that showed a full biochemical breakdown of individual foods, so my search began. After reading many of these texts, it became obvious that several of the pharmacologically active chemicals in medicinal plants that make them medicinal are also present in notable concentrations in culinary plants. That had to be the answer. When we consume a diet that centres on wholefoods, with a high level of fresh plant foods, we are taking advantage of nature's potent medicine cabinet. We are consuming a vast quantity of chemical compounds that deliver some incredible healing actions. These compounds aren't nutrients at all, because they are not *vital* for normal functioning. You can't develop deficiency diseases if you don't consume enough of them. Yet they do have some serious effects upon physiology. What they are is nature's

potent medicinal bonus. They are pharmacologically active medicines!

SO WHY ARE PHYTOCHEMICALS THERE?

Phytochemicals play a myriad of different functions in plants. Some may be vivid, striking colour pigments, such as the deep purple betacyanin found in beetroot, or anthocyanins found in red onions. Others may serve a hormone-like function in the plant or regulate different stages of the plant's growth. Others may become part of the plant's structure or act as a readily available food source for the plant.

When we take all this into consideration, it should strike us as glaringly obvious that the food that we eat every single day can be the most enjoyable form of medicine, or the slowest form of poison. The evidence base is there. The epidemiological data (disease patterns among populations) shows that our diets in the developed world have gone horribly wrong and our general state of health is awful. We are eating ourselves into the doctor's waiting room and an early grave. It is my desire to portray information about how to prevent and reverse this in a way that will allow you to develop a clear and thorough understanding of the science of this subject, and put it to practical use every single day. This book is designed to be a reference book that you can come back to again and again.

MEDICINAL COOKERY
SYSTEM BY SYSTEM

The beauty of understanding phytochemistry, and how nature offers us a delicious pharmacy, is that we can create an abundance of medicinal morsels from the simplest of ingredients. When we understand which foods contain certain chemicals, and how these chemical compounds influence our body's chemistry in order to deliver a healing response, we can get into the kitchen and cook up and create our own medicine.

THE SKIN

If I were to ask you which is the largest organ in the body, I imagine that many of you would say the brain, or the lungs or the liver. Well, believe it or not, it's our skin. Many of us don't think of our skin as an organ, but it is the biggest organ of the human body, weighing an average 2.7 kilograms. As such, it has its own specific and unique nutritional needs and responds to specific nutritional interventions. Getting a grip on these will help you to keep your skin looking fantastic and functioning wonderfully – and will enable you to manage some skin issues effectively.

KEY FUNCTIONS OF THE SKIN

The first and most obvious major function of the skin is to act as a physical barrier to the outside world. All our body's tissues are so delicate that the most microscopic level of exposure to many external elements would be enough to kill us in a short space of time. The skin offers us protection against this. It also keeps everything where it should be. This function is blatantly obvious. However, the array of functions the skin has are really rather impressive.

AN EXTENSION OF THE IMMUNE SYSTEM

The skin is a fully fledged part of our body's immune system. This is partially due to the physical barrier it provides, which keeps pathogens out, but there is more to it than that.

Our skin is covered in a vast community of billions of bacteria. If you were to look at this heavily populated landscape under a microscope, it would blow your mind to see what a sprawling squirming metropolis it is. Several species of bacteria live happily and symbiotically on its surface. We provide a safe environment that is conducive to growth for them, and in return they help us. One of the roles that these tiny passengers can play is a defensive one against certain types of potentially harmful pathogenic bacteria. This can be as a result of direct aggression towards the potential invader, or simply by competing for space on our skin's surface. There is only so much room on the skin and these billions of symbiotic bacteria take up almost all of it. So much so that there is barely any room for others to adhere to the surface to an extent that would cause infection.

The skin can also help the internal immune system in the early stages of detecting a pathogen. There are specialised cells embedded within the skin called Langerhans cells. These cells basically work as surveillance stations in the outer layers of the skin. They can detect specific harmful pathogens and then communicate information to our systemic immunity inside the body, via a sequence of chemical signals that travel through the lymphatic system. These signals warn that trouble is coming, and what form that trouble takes.

TEMPERATURE REGULATION

The skin is the key factor in regulating the temperature of the human body. The surface of the skin is highly sensitive (more on that later) and can detect the slightest change in environmental temperature. It relays this information to our brain's main control centre, the hypothalamus, which defines what the body temperature should be. If internal or environmental factors cause the temperature to deviate outside this point, then the hypothalamus responds to the signal by instigating the relevant responses to make the body warmer or cooler.

If we are too cold, the hypothalamus will send messages to the skin causing it to narrow the capillaries that supply it. This reduces heat loss through the surface of the skin. This is why we tend to look a little pale when we are cold – blood flow is reduced. There is also a signal to the skeletal muscles that cause the body to shiver in order to generate heat.

When we are hot, nerve impulses sent to the skin cause the capillaries that supply the skin to dilate, allowing heat to escape through the skin's surface. The sweat glands are also stimulated and, as the sweat evaporates off the surface of the skin, it cools us down rapidly.

SENSORY ORGAN

The skin is, of course, one of the major sensory organs, delivering the sense of touch. There are thousands of nerve endings within the skin, and some parts of the body (such as the fingertips) have higher concentrations than others. Four main sensations are transmitted through the skin: hot, cold, contact and pain. There are a number of different types of pressure receptor which detect variations in touch, and allow us to determine textures, and so on. The hairs on the skin also play a role in our sensory perception.

VITAMIN D PRODUCTION

One of the most exciting things (well, for a nerd like me at least) that the skin does is manufacture vitamin D when exposed to ultraviolet rays from the sun. It does this by transforming cholesterol into vitamin D3, which is actually a precursor for the active form of this nutrient that requires further conversion by the liver and kidneys. This transformation of cholesterol takes place in two deep areas of the skin: the stratum basale and the stratum spinosum (see below).

STRUCTURE OF THE SKIN

A key to having healthy skin and managing all manner of skin issues is understanding its structure and the complexities of how it works. Once you understand this, you can gauge how nutrition can be applied therapeutically.

THE EPIDERMIS

The epidermis is the outermost layer of the skin; its thickness varies throughout the body. On the soles of the feet and the palms of the hands, the epidermis is about 1–5mm thick. In contrast, the eyelids have an epidermis of 0.5mm. The epidermis is made up of five distinct layers. These are:

- the stratum corneum (the top layer);
- the stratum lucidum;
- the stratum granulosum;
- the stratum spinosum;
- the stratum basale (the bottom layer).

Each layer is made up of different types of cells. The top layer, the stratum corneum, is made up of flat, dead skin cells that regularly slough away and are shed, on average, every two weeks. The bottom layer, the stratum basale, is where new skin cells begin to form. Most of this layer is made up of cells that resemble columns which push growing cells upwards into the other layers of the skin, where they move through the ranks until they reach the stratum corneum, where they are eventually sloughed away.

There are also several types of specialist cell within the epidermis. The first of these are the melanocytes. These are the cells responsible for giving our skin its pigment (melanin) and its lovely summer tan. They are located in the stratum basale, and secrete melanin in response to various stimuli, the main one being exposure to ultraviolet radiation. When melanocytes secrete melanin, they transport it to keratinocytes through a network of dendrites. At its destination, the melanin gives dark coloration to the skin.

The next group of specialised cells in the epidermis are the Langerhans cells. These are involved in identifying potentially pathogenic organisms, and sending signals to other branches of the immune system, as a kind of skin-bound early warning mechanism. They do this by sending chemical messages throughout the lymphatic system, which then warn the white cells of the immune system of the potential onslaught that may be coming. See the chapter on the immune system for more detail on this.

The final group of specialised cells in the epidermis are called merkel cells, but strangely, we have yet to discover exactly what they do!

THE DERMIS

The dermis is the next layer down in the skin's structure. It can be anywhere between ten and forty times thicker than the epidermis. The top part of the dermis is a rocky, bumpy terrain consisting of projections of fibres, blood vessels and nerve endings. This upper layer that meets the epidermis is known as the dermal papillae. The main type of cell in the dermis is called a fibroblast.

The role of this busy cell is the constant manufacture and secretion of the two key structural components of the skin – collagen and elastin. These fibrous protein filaments give the skin its plumpness, firmness and elasticity. These cells are mostly in the very upper layer of the dermis, in the region of the dermal papillae.

The lower part of the dermal papillae is home to a series of microcapillaries. Some of these vessels are found lower down in the dermis too. Their role is to provide oxygen and nutrients to the epidermis, and also to regulate the skin's temperature.

Below the dermal papillae, the deeper parts of the dermis are known as the reticular dermis. This thick tissue, with many criss-crossing collagen and elastin fibres, is also home to the pilosebaceous unit. This structure consists of a hair, the hair follicle, a sebaceous gland and the musculature used to make hairs stand up and relax. It delivers lubrication to the skin in the form of sebum – the oily secretion released by the sebaceous gland. You will see later in this book that this can be the site of some problems. Sweat glands are also found in the reticular dermis, along with a series of ducts that carry sweat up to the dermis during thermoregulation.

THE SUBCUTIS

The subcutis, often called the hypodermis, or subcutaneous layer, is the deepest and thickest part of the skin. This region is composed predominantly of collagen fibres and fat storage cells known as adipocytes. These fatty cells are grouped together in clumps within this layer. The fats contained within the subcutis not only offer us a certain degree of cushioning, but also act as an energy source. It is in this area that we accumulate body fat, from sedentary living or overconsumption of the wrong types of foods. These fats can be put back into circulation as fuel when we are following a weight-management diet or are exercising effectively.

A high number of cells from the immune system, known as macrophages, are also found within the subcutis. These cells are able to identify any pathogens or dysfunctional cells from our body, and completely engulf them. Once they have engulfed them, they quickly break down the invader or damaged cell and remove it. This is a crude but effective first-line defence.

The subcutis is also home to some other larger structures. There is a series of thicker blood vessels that supply the smaller capillaries that run through the dermis. Bundled in with these is a series of lymphatic vessels that lead from the other two layers of the skin. These vessels carry away waste material created from normal metabolic processes; they can filter out some pathogenic material too.

The final group of structures housed in the subcutis are the nerve structures. Nervous tissue runs throughout all the layers of the skin, with the nerve endings being at the top of the epidermis – these allow us to touch and feel the world around us. The subcutis is where this nervous tissue begins to bundle together. Some unique neurological structures also reside here, including the pacinian corpuscle. This is a type of nerve receptor that detects pressure and vibration.

COMMON SKIN CONDITIONS

This is not an exhaustive list of skin conditions, but these are the three big ones that definitely draw upon diet as part of the treatment protocol.

ACNE

Acne is an inflammatory disorder that occurs in the pilosebacous unit. This is the area where the sebaceous gland and hair follicle meet. The first stage in the process of an acne lesion (spot) forming is the stimulation of the sebaceous gland to secrete a more viscous sebum (oil) by androgen hormones (such as testosterone). When this viscous sebum is secreted, it can begin to trap things in the pore. The hormonal profiles that cause sebaceous stimulation also spark an excessive shedding of keratinocytes (an epidermal cell that produces the structural material keratin). The combination of trapped keratinocytes and viscous sebum blocks the pore. At this stage the bacteria *Propionibacterium acnes* that usually lives quite happily in the follicle becomes trapped and begins to trigger an inflammatory response. During this inflammatory episode, the follicle can become damaged and the contents of the pore can begin to leach into surrounding tissue, which further triggers the inflammatory cascade. Before you know it you have raised redness, and as inflammation and infection ensues, the characteristic pus-filled whitehead occurs.

ECZEMA

This inflammatory condition of the skin is sometimes also referred to as atopic dermatitis. Atopic refers to genetic susceptibility to allergic reactions. Eczema usually goes hand in hand with asthma and hay fever, and sometimes individuals can be afflicted by two or more of these at once. Skin that is eczema-prone tends to produce less oil and retain less moisture than normal skin. It is believed that this drier skin may have less physical barrier protection against things that could irritate the skin. Whatever is happening, the flare-ups experienced are related to acute inflammation of the skin. In mild cases this inflammation causes redness and itching. In more severe cases the inflamed skin can weep, bleed and become crusty.

PSORIASIS

Psoriasis is an autoimmune condition, meaning that for whatever reason, the body's immune system is reacting to its own tissue, causing damage. In psoriasis it is believed that an immunological response by several lines of immunological cells releases chemicals that instigate an inflammatory cascade in the dermis. This causes the premature ageing of different types of skin cells and the natural process of new skin cell production goes haywire. There is an accelerated growth of the epidermis. Skin cells are usually replaced every 28–30 days. In psoriasis this speeds up to every 3–5 days. This sequence of events causes a lesion that begins as irritated redness (the inflammation) and then changes to a lesion that is raised and scaly. The scales are a silvery colour, with patches of redness surrounding the lesion. As the lesion develops, the itching and discomfort can drive the sufferer to distraction.

THERAPEUTIC MANAGEMENT OF SKIN CONDITIONS

I know from experience just how distressing skin lesions can be. Our skin, especially on our face, hands and arms, is on constant display to the outside world. This is one of the most personally distressing types of disorder that can affect us. In general, whatever the root cause and trigger, skin conditions come down to two distinct factors – infection and inflammation. Acne is, of course, a prime example of both these elements in action. When infection arises in a blocked pore, localised inflammation ensues. If we learn natural ways to manage both these responses, we can have a huge impact upon both the appearance and future development of skin disorders.

REGULATING INFLAMMATION

Almost all skin lesions, regardless of their cause, involve inflammation. Eczema is a perfect example of an inflammatory condition. It is what we call a type 2 hyper-sensitivity reaction. This basically means that the body's own immune system has become overly sensitised to a specific stimulus. This could be a food, or something in the local environment such as a detergent or pollut-ant. Whenever the immune system comes into contact with this specific stimulus, it delivers a normal immunological response, but in a far more aggressive way than is necessary. This then causes inflammation in the upper layers of the skin, and the typical eczema lesion of raised, red, itchy patches ensues. Also, think about acne. The inflam-mation in the pilosebaceous unit is what leads to the redness and the angry-looking

lesion. By reducing inflammation we can make the lesion look far less severe and also help calm pain and irritation.

There are many foods that can help the body to reduce its inflammatory load. Some of these foods interrupt normal chemical reactions that switch on inflammation. Others manipulate the production of biochemicals that regulate the rate and extent of inflammation in the body.

KEY FOODS FOR REDUCING INFLAMMATION

OILY FISH

Oily fish such as salmon, mackerel, herring, tuna and sardines are top of the list when it comes to foods to fight inflammation. This is because they are packed with special types of fats called omega 3 fatty acids. These vitamin-like, fat-derived compounds basically work as either structural components in the body, or as the precursors to chemicals that regulate various processes in the body. It is in this context that they become anti-inflammatory heroes. Omega 3 fatty acids found in fish – called EPA and DHA – are the precursors to a group of compounds called prostaglandins that regulate the inflammatory response in the body. There are three types of prostaglandins – series

1, series 2 and series 3. Series 1 and 3 prostaglandins switch off inflammation, whereas series 2 prostaglandins switch it on and exacerbate it. By consuming increased amounts of EPA and DHA from oily fish, we feed more and more of them into the biochemical pathways that create series 1 and 3 prostaglandins – the anti-inflammatory ones. We can force-feed the body so it creates more anti-inflammatory compounds, and their influence on inflammatory issues is profound. Omega 3 fatty acids are without doubt *the* most powerful dietary influencers of inflammation.

GINGER

Ginger has long been revered as an anti-inflammatory. There is certainly an element of truth to this. Compounds in ginger, such as gingerols, have been shown to influence inflammation. They do this by interfering with the biochemical pathway that makes prostaglandins. Now, as discussed above, there are three types of prostaglandin. Series 1 and 3 switch off inflammation, and series 2 switches on inflammation. Fatty acids such as EPA are converted into the anti-inflammatory pros-taglandins. A fatty acid called arachidonic acid is converted into the series 2 pros-taglandins that switch *on* inflammation. There is an enzyme called cyclooxygenase that is involved in the conversion of arachi-donic acid into the series 2 prostaglandin. Gingerols have been shown to reduce the

activity of cyclooxygenase in clinical trials using extracts of ginger.

PINEAPPLE

Pineapple contains a very potent enzyme called bromelain. Similar to the active con-stituents in ginger, bromelain can interfere with the conversion of arachidonic acid into series 2 prostaglandins. This potent enzyme is found in the tough central core of the pineapple – the bit that many of us throw away!

REGULATING OIL PRODUCTION

Sebum, the natural oil found in our skin and produced in tiny glands within hair follicles, is a vital factor for skin health. It regulates moisture levels, offers protection against age-related damage and also makes the skin waterproof. In normal circumstances, we are generally unaware that it is there. However, those with oily, acne-prone skin or those with excessively dry skin will be acutely aware of the impact it can have upon the health of the skin. It is sebum that is the main cause of spot formation. If our sebum fills pores in the skin to a certain level, and is at a certain viscosity, it can begin to oxidise – especially if it fills the pore to the extent that it comes into contact with air. When this occurs, it begins to toughen, turns a dark colour, and a comedo or blackhead is formed. Blackheads then become a collection site for bacteria such as staphylococcus, which live naturally and harmlessly on the outer surface of the skin. When such bacteria collect around a comedo, it eventually sets off an infection, and, hey presto, a spot forms.

Many factors in our bodies can affect sebum and what it does. The hormone testosterone, for example, can aggravate and drastically increase the production of sebum. Testosterone also makes the sebum more viscous, so more likely to block the pore and cause infection.

Zinc is an important mineral involved in dozens of enzymatic reactions in the body. One of the interesting properties of zinc is regulating sebaceous secretions. If the skin is too oily, adequate zinc in the diet can tone down oil secretions. Conversely, if the skin is very dry then adequate zinc intake can increase oil production. So in essence it balances oil in the skin.

FIGHTING INFECTION

In acne, infection is the single thing that causes these painful and unpleasant lesions. Infection arises as viscous sebaceous secretions trap bacteria that naturally live on the skin in the pore. The immune system soon responds to this and causes localised inflammation in the pore, and before you know it, a spot has formed. Any means of fighting infection will help to clear these lesions faster.

KEY FOODS FOR FIGHTING INFECTION

SHELLFISH

Shellfish, especially prawns, are a great source of the mineral zinc. This vital mineral is used by the white blood cells of the immune system to code genes that then programme the way in which they deal with specific pathogens and fight infection.

PUMPKIN SEEDS

These are a great zinc-rich food for vegetarians.

SHIITAKE MUSHROOMS

Shiitake mushrooms are one of my favourite ingredients that influence the immune system. Greater detail about these is given in the chapter on the immune system, but the long and short of it is that they contain a specialised type of sugar called a polysaccharide. These polysaccharides have been shown in over forty years of clinical study to increase the production of certain lines of white blood cells that can increase our infection-fighting capacity.

PROTECTING KEY STRUCTURES

One of the greatest things we can do to achieve healthy-looking skin for life is to protect some of the key underlying structures in the skin from the damage that we associate with premature ageing. If you recall, in the deeper layers of the skin there are some structures that give the skin its structural integrity. Structural proteins such as collagen and elastin, for example, help our skin to stay supple, youthful and wrinkle free. Natural degradation of these structures over time is a natural part of the ageing process. While there is nothing that can stop ageing indefinitely, our diet and lifestyle can have a huge impact upon the rate and the extent to which this natural degradation occurs. With this in mind, understanding a few key ways in which our diet can influence this, we can do a lot to help ourselves keep our skin healthy and youthful.

KEY FOODS FOR PROTECTING KEY STRUCTURES

ORANGE FRUITS AND VEGETABLES

Orange fruits and vegetables such as butternut squash, sweet potatoes, carrots, mangoes and melons are a highly important part of your protective armoury against premature ageing of the skin. This is because they are very rich in a group of compounds called carotenoids – the compounds that give them their distinctive orange colour pigment. Carotenoids are fat-soluble antioxidants. There are tens of thousands of substances that potentially have antioxidant activity. We hear people talking about antioxidants all the time, and rarely do they seem to believe that they all do the same thing. You will see articles in glossy magazines telling you that X or Y ingredient is packed with antioxidants and is therefore wonderful for the skin. This is far too simplistic a view. There is such vast variation in what antioxidants do and in which types of tissue that lumping them together is just daft.

That being said, antioxidants can generally be placed into two distinct categories – water soluble and fat soluble. Water-soluble antioxidants, such as vitamin C, are taken into systemic circulation and deliver their activity, are metabolised and excreted within a specific time frame. Fat-soluble antioxidants, on the other hand, don't want to be in our systemic circulation. By their very nature they want to migrate into fatty tissues. Second to the brain, the most abundant fatty tissue in the body is in the subcutaneous layer of the skin. So when we consume enough fat-soluble antioxidants, we can have an accumulation of them in the skin. There is even a condition called hypercarotenemia, in which carotenoids accumulated in the skin give the skin an orange colour (perhaps this goes some way to explain *The Only Way is Essex* . . . hmmm). This is testament to the ability of fat-soluble antioxidants to accumulate. This accumulation means that they can deliver antioxidant activity at a local level. They can protect structures such as collagen and elastin fibres from oxidative damage – something that ages them prematurely.

VITAMIN C RICH FOODS

Vitamin C is important, but not because of its antioxidant activity. As explained, this is delivered systemically. Vitamin C is, however, an important cofactor in the manufacture of collagen. When combined with taking action against collagen degradation, the results can be quite staggering. Spinach, peppers, mangoes, kiwi fruit – and of course citrus fruit – are all great sources.

RECIPES FOR SKIN HEALTH
– TOP INGREDIENTS –

The recipes that follow contain ingredients which have medicinal properties that benefit skin health. Here is a rundown of why they are 'star' ingredients, along with their medicinal properties:

AVOCADO (pages 38, 41) is a great source of the fat-soluble antioxidant vitamin E. In terms of skin health, vitamin E can help to protect skin cell membranes from free radical damage. It also keeps skin cell membranes healthier and can help to keep the skin looking plump, as well as reducing moisture loss.

BUTTERNUT SQUASH (pages 41, 44) is a delicious anti-inflammatory food. Its rich orange flesh is bursting with the plant pigment beta-carotene, the same as that found in carrots. This delivers powerful anti-inflammatory activity. It also supplies a huge boost in vitamin A, which helps to regulate oil production in the skin, and gives it a more youthful appearance.

CARROTS (pages 35, 37) are a great source of the fat-soluble antioxidant beta-carotene. This can accumulate in the subcutaneous layer of the skin, offering localised protection to key structures there.

CHICKPEAS (page 44) are one of my staples. I can't get enough of them! From a nutritional perspective, they are very high in fibre, which helps to clear waste out of the digestive tract. This in itself can give the skin an extra glow. They are also very high in zinc, so can be a good aid to skin healing. Chickpeas are also rich in a rare trace mineral called molybdenum, which among other things can assist in the breakdown of certain environmental and metabolic toxins in the liver.

GINGER (pages 35, 37, 44) is a wonderful and versatile spice that contains compounds such as gingerols, which have been shown to reduce the enzyme activity that contributes to inflammation.

ONIONS AND GARLIC (pages 35, 36, 42, 44, 45, 46) are rich sources of sulphur, which can help to keep the skin looking smooth and taut by strengthening bonds between skin cells.

PRAWNS (page 42) are packed with infection-fighting zinc. Zinc helps white blood cells to regulate the way in which they respond to infection and is also important in regulating sebaceous gland activity - which helps to even out oil production.

PEPPERS (pages 36, 46) are a rich source of carotenoids, which have a strong anti-oxidant quality, which has been linked with increased protection against cancers.

RAINBOW CHARD (page 44) is a very close relative of the humble beetroot. It contains a good level of a compound called betacyanin, which is the red pigment found in the stems and veins of these delicious leaves. Betacyanin is known to speed up certain functions within the liver that break down toxic matter and prepare it for removal from the body. This particular function is a series of chemical processes known as phase 2 detoxification, which is the second stage of processing the liver uses before sending processed toxins to either the kidneys or bowel. Enhancing such processes can help the skin in the long run, as it keeps levels of toxic waste down.

SALMON (pages 37, 38) is an excellent source of preformed EPA and DHA omega 3 fatty acids. These are some of the best nutrients for inflammatory skin lesions such as acne, eczema and psoriasis. This is because they directly target the inflammation, due to the fact that they are converted into anti-inflammatory compounds called series 1 and 3 prostaglandins, resolvins and protectins. In short, they won't get rid of the lesions, but will help to tone down the redness and swelling, so will reduce the severity of their appearance and any discomfort.

SWEET POTATO (pages 36, 38, 45, 46) The bright orange flesh of sweet potatoes is given by beta carotene, the plant form of vitamin A. This is one of those all important fat-soluble antioxidants that have been so widely discussed in this chapter. Accumulating in the subcutaneous layers of the skin, it offers localised anti-inflammatory protection.

CLASSIC CARROT AND GINGER SOUP

SERVES 4

5cm piece ginger, peeled and
    finely chopped
2 cloves garlic, finely chopped
2 sticks celery, thinly sliced
1 red onion, finely chopped
olive oil, for frying
5 large carrots, skin on,
    coarsely chopped
1 large baking potato, skin
    on, coarsely chopped
vegetable stock
sea salt

This recipe is both a classic and a real winter warmer. It is wonderful for anyone fighting a skin disorder, as it offers tremendous support from both a nutritional and a medicinal perspective.

1. In a saucepan, sauté the ginger, garlic, celery and onion in a little olive oil with a pinch of salt until the onion is softened.

2. Add the chopped carrot and potato, and enough stock to just cover them. Simmer until the vegetables are almost soft, then blend into a smooth, bright orange soup.

MEDICINAL PROPERTIES

CARROTS
GINGER
ONIONS AND GARLIC

ROASTED RED PEPPER AND SWEET POTATO SOUP

SERVES 2

1 red onion, coarsely
   chopped
2 cloves of garlic, finely
   chopped
olive oil, for frying
3 red peppers, coarsely
   chopped
1 large sweet potato, diced
sea salt
300ml vegetable stock

This luscious thick soup is packed with skin-loving ingredients. It is like a carotenoid bath.

1. Sauté the onion and garlic in a little olive oil, along with a good pinch of sea salt, until the onion has softened.

2. Add the red peppers and diced sweet potato, and enough vegetable stock to cover the vegetables.

3. Simmer until the sweet potato has softened.

4. Blend into a smooth soup.

MEDICINAL PROPERTIES

ONIONS AND GARLIC
PEPPERS
SWEET POTATO

MISO GINGER SALMON WITH CARROT AND CARAWAY PURÉE

SERVES 2

1 heaped teaspoon miso
  paste
1 teaspoon honey
2 teaspoons sesame oil
½ teaspoon grated ginger
2 salmon fillets
4 large carrots, sliced in
  rounds
1 teaspoon caraway seeds
sea salt

MEDICINAL PROPERTIES

CARROTS
GINGER
SALMON

This is a beautifully flavoured dish that really makes these skin-healthy ingredients sing.

1. In a bowl mix the miso paste, honey, sesame oil and grated ginger to create a marinade. Put the salmon fillets into a shallow dish and cover them with the marinade. Leave for 2–3 hours.

2. Preheat the oven to 180°C/160°C fan/350°F/gas mark 4. Put the marinated salmon fillets on an oiled baking sheet, and bake for about 20 minutes.

3. While the salmon is cooking, place the sliced carrots and caraway seeds in a saucepan, and add enough water to half cover the carrots. Simmer until they are soft, season with a little salt and then purée using a stick blender or food processor.

4. Spoon a generous dollop of the purée into the centre of each plate, and top with a salmon fillet.

ROASTED SWEET POTATO, SMOKED SALMON, GOATS' CHEESE AND WALNUT SALAD

SERVES 1

½ medium sweet potato,
  skin on, diced
olive oil to drizzle
2 handfuls mixed salad leaves
1 fillet hot smoked salmon
½ avocado, diced
Handful of walnuts, chopped
75g goats' cheese
sea salt

for the dressing
1 teaspoon balsamic vinegar
1 tablespoon olive oil
¼ tablespoon mixed herbs
pinch of salt

This gorgeous, filling salad is packed to the hilt with vital nutrients for skin health.

1. Preheat the oven to 180°C/160°C fan/350°F/gas mark 4. Place the diced sweet potato on a roasting tray. Drizzle with olive oil and a pinch of salt and roast for 20–25 minutes. Turn occasionally.

2. Whisk all the dressing ingredients together into a thick vinaigrette.

3. Assemble the salad by placing the leaves in a salad bowl, breaking up the salmon fillet over the leaves, adding the diced avocado, walnuts and sweet potato, crumbling over the goats' cheese, then drizzling the dressing over them all.

MEDICINAL PROPERTIES

AVOCADO
SALMON
SWEET POTATO

SQUASH CROQUETTES WITH MINTED AVOCADO DIPPING SAUCE

**MAKES ABOUT
15 CROQUETTES**

½ medium butternut squash,
   peeled and diced
200g chickpea flour
2 spring onions, finely
   chopped
small bunch flat leaf parsley,
   finely chopped
50g feta cheese
Panko crumbs (enough to
   coat a plate)
sea salt and pepper

for the dipping sauce
1 very ripe avocado
3 tablespoons olive oil
juice of half a lime
10g fresh mint
sea salt and pepper

MEDICINAL PROPERTIES

AVOCADO
BUTTERNUT SQUASH

These are an awesome little finger snack, perfect for munching in front of the TV or as a canapé.

1. Place the diced squash in a saucepan, and cover with boiling water. Simmer until the squash is soft and can be mashed. Preheat the oven to 180°C/160°C fan/350°F/gas mark 4.

2. Drain the squash and leave to cool down in a colander for a few minutes. Then mash it with a potato masher. Add small amounts of chickpea flour in increments and mix well until a stiff dough forms that you can easily work by hand. Add the spring onions and parsley. Crumble in the feta cheese, taste to check seasoning and if necessary add some salt and pepper.

3. Roll the dough into sausages and cut them into 2–3cm long croquettes.

4. Sprinkle the panko crumbs on a plate and roll the croquettes through them to ensure a good coating. Place them on a baking tray, and bake for 20–25 minutes, or until golden brown.

5. While the croquettes are cooking, make the sauce. Scoop the avocado flesh into a food processor. Add the olive oil, lime juice, mint and a pinch of salt and pepper. Blitz into a smooth dip.

PRAWNS AND GREENS IN SATAY SAUCE

SERVES 2

2 cloves garlic, finely chopped
1 large red onion, halved,
   then thinly sliced
1 small leek, thinly sliced
1 small red chilli, chopped
olive oil, for frying
100g cavolo nero, roughly
   chopped
180g cooked king prawns
1 heaped tablespoon smooth
   peanut butter
2 teaspoons soy sauce
1 teaspoon honey
½ teaspoon Chinese five
   spice
small sprig coriander, roughly
   chopped
sea salt

I spend a lot of time in Asia, and this dish brings together all my favourite flavours.

1. In a frying pan stir-fry the garlic, onion, leek and chilli in the olive oil, along with a pinch of salt, until the onion and leek have softened.

2. Add the cavolo nero and continue to stir-fry until it has wilted.

3. Add the king prawns, peanut butter, soy sauce, honey and Chinese five spice and mix well. Cook for another minute or so, before adding the chopped coriander.

MEDICINAL PROPERTIES

ONIONS AND GARLIC
PRAWNS

CHICKPEA, SQUASH AND RAINBOW CHARD CURRY

SERVES 4

2 cloves garlic, finely chopped
1 red onion, finely chopped
2.5cm piece fresh ginger,
  peeled and finely chopped
Olive oil, for frying
2 tablespoons Thai green
  curry paste
250g butternut squash, skin
  on, cubed
400g can chickpeas, drained
1 heaped tablespoon
  peanut butter
300ml coconut milk
120ml vegetable stock
2 large bunches rainbow
  chard, shredded

This simple curry tastes wonderful and is a real nutrient bomb.

1. Fry the garlic, onion and ginger in a saucepan with a little oil until the onion starts to turn a lighter colour.

2. Add the curry paste and continue to sauté until the mixture becomes highly fragrant.

3. Add the squash, chickpeas and peanut butter, and mix well.

4. Pour in the coconut milk and the stock. Simmer gently for about 30 minutes, until the squash becomes tender.

5. Add the rainbow chard and cook until it wilts. Serve the curry with a side salad.

MEDICINAL PROPERTIES

BUTTERNUT SQUASH
CHICKPEAS
GINGER
ONIONS AND GARLIC
RAINBOW CHARD

SWEET POTATO AND WHITE BEAN STEW

SERVES 2

1 large red onion, finely
   chopped
2 cloves garlic, finely chopped
olive oil, for frying
2 teaspoons miso paste
1 large sweet potato, skin on,
   diced
400g can butter beans,
   drained
sea salt

This delicious warming dish is fantastic for the colder months. Filling and rich.

1. In a saucepan sauté the onion and garlic in olive oil with a pinch of salt until the onion softens.

2. Add the miso paste, sweet potato and butter beans. Mix well.

3. Add enough water to half cover the contents of the pan and then allow to simmer for 20 minutes, or until the sweet potato has softened. Add more water in small increments if necessary, but aim for a thick, rich stew.

MEDICINAL PROPERTIES

ONIONS AND GARLIC
SWEET POTATO

SWEET POTATO GNOCCHI WITH BABY SPINACH AND RED PEPPER SAUCE

SERVES 2

1 large sweet potato, peeled and diced
120g wholemeal flour
2 large red peppers, deseeded and halved
½ red onion, finely chopped
1 clove garlic, finely chopped
olive oil, for frying
2 handfuls baby spinach
sea salt and pepper

MEDICINAL PROPERTIES

ONIONS AND GARLIC
PEPPERS
SWEET POTATO

This simplified version of gnocchi is super easy, and the red pepper sauce has some serious flavour to it. This dish is a pure antioxidant bath for the skin.

1. Place the diced sweet potato in a saucepan, cover with boiling water and simmer until it is soft. Drain and leave to cool for a few minutes before mashing.

2. Preheat the oven to 180°C/160°C fan/350°F/gas mark 4.

3. Begin adding flour to the mash until a dough forms that can be worked by hand. Season with salt and pepper and then roll the dough into long sausages about 2.5cm across. Cut the sausages into small, bite-size gnocchi. Place on a plate and keep in the fridge while you make the sauce.

4. Place the pepper halves on a baking tray and bake for about 30 minutes. Ovens vary, so keep an eye on them. Aim for soft peppers that are beginning to blacken and blister in places.

5. While the peppers are roasting, sauté the onion and garlic in a saucepan with a little olive oil along with a good pinch of salt, until the onion has softened.

cont.

6. Put the peppers, onion and garlic in a food processor and blitz them into a coarse, vibrant-tasting sauce. Return it to the pan.

7. Take the gnocchi out of the fridge and put them in another saucepan. Cover with boiling water and simmer until the gnocchi float to the top of the water. Fish them out with a slotted spoon.

8. Put the cooked gnocchi in the sauce and cook on a high heat. As the sauce starts to get hot, add the spinach and continue to cook until it has wilted.

GENERAL TIPS TO REMEMBER FOR SKIN HEALTH

STAY HYDRATED. This is important to skin health for two main reasons. First, hydrated skin has fewer fine lines, better elasticity and looks generally brighter. Second, drinking plenty of water helps to flush out water-soluble toxins from the kidneys. Remember that the skin will be used as a fast and convenient waste removal system if any of the other modes of elimination are in any way inhibited. This can lead to skin breakouts and lesions. However, don't overdo it and drink excessive amounts of water. That can be dangerous and even lead to death.

GET THE BEST SKINCARE POSSIBLE. A good skincare regime can work wonders for the way skin functions and thrives as an organ, and is essential for those with skin complaints. Choose products with the minimum of harsh chemicals and get advice from an expert to find ones that are best for you.

REDUCE SUGAR INTAKE. When we eat sugar, we get a very sudden rise in blood sugar. When this happens, the body initially releases adrenalin (hence the sugar rush). After adrenalin has surged round the body for a while, the body will start to release insulin, in order to tell the cells to suck in the excess sugar and get it out of the bloodstream. When we have high levels of adrenalin in circulation, the skin is affected, as adrenalin directly stimulates the sebaceous glands in the skin. This causes a drastic increase in the production of sebum, and increases the likelihood of developing skin breakouts.

FILL UP ON FAT. Now, before you get excited and phone the local pizza joint, I am talking about the good fats: omegas 3, 6 and 9. These fats are vital for skin health. They help to condition the skin and control inflammation. Also, many of the food sources of these fats are very rich in other important nutrients such as zinc and vitamin E. Reach for sources such as hemp seeds, pumpkin seeds, algae spirulina and oily fish (if you are happy to eat it).

THE DIGESTIVE SYSTEM

The digestive system is undoubtedly one of the most used and abused of body systems. Consisting of the digestive tract (the hollow tube that runs from mouth to anus), the liver and the pancreas, the digestive system is the gateway for the abundance of beautiful foods out there to nourish us and help us grow and evolve. There are many common digestive issues, all of which tend to have very different causes. I have written a detailed book on digestion – *Digestion: Eat Your Way to Better Health* – that goes into greater depth about specific ailments and their management. As that is so specialised, this chapter will deal with general overall digestive health and how to support and maintain it.

THE JOURNEY THROUGH THE DIGESTIVE TRACT

Digestion starts in the mouth. Our teeth mechanically break down large pieces of food so as to increase the surface area for digestive enzymes to act upon further along the digestive tract. There are also some simple carbohydrate-digesting enzymes in our saliva that start off the process. These enzymes, such as salivary amylase, help to liberate some of the more freely available simple sugars that are not bound tightly in fibre or within cells. A perfect example is white bread. Chew a piece of white bread and it gets sweeter and sweeter. As there is very little fibre, the sugars can be liberated rapidly by the salivary amylase. It is this rapid liberation that causes the bread to taste sweeter within a few seconds.

The next stop is the stomach. This is a highly acidic environment that churns food

round and round to assist its breakdown. The stomach is the primary location for protein digestion. Using digestive fluids such as pepsin and hydrochloric acid, proteins begin to be broken down into their individual amino-acid components. These fluids also help to kill any nasty bacteria that may have been lurking in our food.

Once the stomach has done its work, the food is then sent on to the small intestine. The intestine is an alkaline environment, so as soon as the acidic chyme (the acidic, partially digested foodstuff that leaves the stomach) enters the intestine, bile salts are released from the liver to buffer the acid, and small spurts of enzymes are released from the pancreas. The small intestine doesn't secrete any of its own digestive fluids, so relies solely on those produced by the pancreas and the liver. These enzymes help to digest dietary fats and carbohydrates, and break them down into small enough units for our body to absorb. Lining the walls of the intestine are billions of tiny finger-like projections known as villi. These little projections are porous and absorb digested food and nutrients, then carry them in the blood to our liver. It takes about three to five hours for the food that leaves our stomach to become a thin, watery nutrient soup. Anything that cannot be absorbed by the villi then makes its way to the large intestine.

The large intestine, or colon, is the final stage of the digestive journey. The watery leftovers that exit the small intestine slowly move through the large intestine where most of the water goes through the colon wall into the bloodstream. As this occurs, the leftover waste material gets harder and harder until a solid mass is formed – and nature's call ensues.

SUPPORTING EVERYDAY GUT HEALTH WITH FOOD

IMPROVE DIGESTIVE TRANSIT

One of the most important and obvious factors in digestive health is healthy digestive transit. Constipation is a huge issue in the Western world. In my own clinical practice, it isn't uncommon for me to see patients who don't go to the loo for two, three, four days or more. That's not a good picture. In an ideal world we should be going after each meal! Regular transit ensures the removal of waste products from the body. A great many of these are from the liver; old cells and metabolic by-products are broken down by the liver and sent to the bowel for removal. If faecal matter stays in the large intestine for too long, then our gut microflora will begin fermenting complex carbohydrates and other food waste. This can cause gas and bloating and considerable digestive discomfort. So ensuring good digestive transit is important, and thankfully really quite easy.

The place to start is fibre! It is important because it has the capacity to take on many times its own weight in water, which causes it to swell in the digestive tract. When it swells, the stool becomes bulkier, which causes the walls of the digestive tract to stretch. Within the walls of the gut there are stretch receptors that detect this gentle stretching as our stool bulks out. When the receptors detect stretch, they in turn stimulate peristalsis. This is the rhythmic contraction of the gut walls that pushes everything along to its final destination!

Far too many of us today are living on beige, highly refined foods. White bread sandwiches, pastries, white rice, white pasta and very little fruit and veg. These foods contain minimal amounts of fibre and have little capacity to take on water and swell up. This can seriously affect peristalsis, so things can just . . . hang around. So the key is to move over to wholefoods. That basically means making sure that the food you eat is as close to its natural state as possible. This isn't weird or idealistic. Just think brown rice instead of white, keep the skins on sweet potatoes, cook vegetables lightly so they still have crunch. That's all it means: wholesome foods that haven't had the living daylights processed out of them. A wholefood diet brings with it a great deal more fibre.

The second part, once you have upped your fibre intake, is that you need to make sure you drink enough water. Fibre works because it takes on water in order to expand. If your total fluid intake is a couple of espressos and a can of something fizzy, you will be doing yourself a great disservice and be in a predicament similar to one in which you have no fibre in your diet. Aim to drink a good-size glass of water every half hour until you notice your urine beginning to run clear when you go to the toilet. At that point stop (too much can leach water-soluble nutrients from the body). When the urine begins to get some colour back, have another decent glass. Continuing like this will keep you well hydrated and, most importantly, provide enough water to get that fibre swelling up to keep your digestion moving!

NURTURE GUT FLORA

Our gut flora is the diverse colony of beneficial bacteria that lives happily within our digestive tract. At any one time there can be between 300 and 1,000. All these play different roles and dwell in different areas of the gut. So what is the purpose of these bacteria? Why are they there? Well, the relationship is a symbiotic and mutually beneficial one. We provide an environment where the bacteria can flourish and feed; they assist us in regulating many aspects of our health. A fair exchange! They help to break down certain types of carbohydrates that cannot be digested higher up in the digestive tract. The gut flora use a process called saccarolytic fermentation to break down these types of carbohydrate. When they do this, a group of by-products is released called short chain fatty acids. These have several functions, such as assisting with nutrient absorption and, most importantly in my opinion, the stimulation of localised repair mechanisms in the lower gut. So a healthy gut flora is like a well-oiled maintenance team. Keep them in good working order!

Things really start getting interesting when we look at the way in which the gut flora interacts with our immune system. This is covered in the immune system chapter, but let's visit it here. Our gut is lined with areas of lymphatic tissue which contains large numbers of white blood cells that act almost like a surveillance station and intermediary between the gut and the rest of the body. The gut is an obvious route for opportunistic pathogens to gain entry into the body, so these offshoots of the immune system are an obvious necessity. We have found in recent years that gut flora can communicate with the rest of our immune system throughout the body via these branches. It is very early days, and the full extent to which this can benefit us remains to be seen, but it is clear that our gut flora does influence immunity. Gut flora also help to regulate peristalsis and can ease, reduce or prevent bloating.

There are some key components in food that can have a positive effect upon gut flora. Certain types of carbohydrate, as described above, require fermentation to break down. These carbohydrates, such as inulin and FOS (fructo-oligosaccharide – a specialised sugar) will actually 'feed' the bacteria when they ferment it, and this whole process helps the bacterial colony grow and flourish. Foods such as onions, leeks, garlic, pulses, and so on are all very rich sources of these, so their regular inclusion in the diet is advised.

RECIPES FOR DIGESTIVE HEALTH
– TOP INGREDIENTS –

The recipes that follow contain ingredients which have medicinal properties that benefit digestive health. Here is a rundown of why they are 'star' ingredients, along with their medicinal properties:

CHIA SEEDS (page 59) are little seeds packed with soluble fibre. You may notice that when they get wet they begin to form a jelly-like texture, even becoming like frog-spawn if you allow them to swell enough. The soluble fibre swells in the digestive tract, taking on many times its weight in water. This makes the contents of the digestive tract increase in size, which causes a stretching of the gut wall. When this occurs, stretch receptors in the gut wall respond by stimulating peristalsis – the rhythmic contraction of the gut wall – that acts to push the gut contents along their way!

FIGS (page 59) are rich in both soluble and insoluble fibre, which, as discussed above, is essential for good gut health.

HERBS (page 64) like bay leaves, caraway seeds, fennel seeds, dried liquorice root and peppermint are all rich in volatile oils that cause relaxation of the gut wall, which helps to break down and dispel gas.

JERUSALEM ARTICHOKES (page 60) are a very rich source of a special type of sugar called inulin. This cannot be broken down higher up in the digestive tract as other more simple sugars can. It requires fermentation by our gut bacteria in order to be partially broken down. This fermentation delivers several benefits. First, it allows gut flora to grow and to flourish. Second, as our gut flora break down and ferment inulin, they release several by-products. One of these is a substance called butyric acid that can stimulate repair mechanisms to the gut lining, helping to keep everything in good working order.

LEEKS (page 63) and all of the aliums, such as garlic and onions, are a very rich source of dietary inulin, the large sugar that requires fermentation by gut flora and serves as a food source and supports growth of the bacterial colony as well as instigating repair mechanisms in the digestive tract.

ONIONS AND GARLIC (pages 60, 65), as with leeks, above, are a rich source of a substance called inulin, which is a prebiotic. This means that it acts as a food source for the good bacteria that resides in the digestive tract. By feeding on prebiotics, this bacterial colony can grow and flourish. Strengthening them is important as they
are involved in regulating almost every aspect of digestive health, from breaking down certain food components, regulating peristalsis, and even triggering repair mechanisms in the gut wall. The role of gut flora goes even further though, having a role to play in immunity, which is discussed in the relevant chapter of this book.

RED LENTILS (page 65) contain both soluble and insoluble fibre. This high fibre content will help to stimulate peristalsis. This increases the volume of gut contents, which causes the gut wall to stretch. Within the gut wall are stretch receptors that detect this stretching. When these receptors are stimulated, they instigate peristalsis, the rhythmical contractions of the gut wall that move gut contents along to . . . its final destination.

SWEET POTATOES (page 63) are rich in another specialised sugar called FOS (fructo-oligosaccharide). Similar to inulin, this is a sugar that is fermented and broken down by our gut flora. As it is broken down it feeds and supports the growth of the bacterial colony.

FIG AND CHIA BARS

MAKES 9

150g dried figs
80g porridge oats
60g sunflower seeds
40g pumpkin seeds
80g chia seeds
80g coconut oil
50g honey

MEDICINAL PROPERTIES
CHIA SEEDS
FIGS

These simple little bars are packed with soluble and insoluble fibre, and make a great breakfast on the run.

1. Roughly chop the figs into small pieces and transfer to a large bowl. Add the oats and seeds and combine thoroughly.

2. In a saucepan, melt the coconut oil and honey together.

3. Transfer the oat, seed and fig mixture to a food processor. Add the melted oil and honey and pulse everything together to form a rough dough.

4. Press the dough into a square tin, and refrigerate for 3–4 hours until fully set. Slice into bars. You can make these any size you want.

ROASTED JERUSALEM ARTICHOKE, RED ONION AND FETA SALAD

SERVES 2

300g Jerusalem artichokes, skins on, quartered longwise
olive oil to drizzle
1 large red onion, cut into thin wedges
2 large handfuls mixed salad leaves
80g feta cheese
sea salt and pepper

for the dressing
½ clove garlic, finely chopped
1 teaspoon apple cider vinegar
1½ tablespoons olive oil
½ teaspoon oregano

MEDICINAL PROPERTIES

JERUSALEM ARTICHOKES
ONIONS AND GARLIC

This is a beautifully flavoured salad. Jerusalem artichokes are strange vegetables. They are not artichokes and have nothing to do with Jerusalem, but they are worth seeking out as their benefit to digestive health is really something. I just apologise for the effects that some people may experience in the early days after consuming them.

1. Preheat the oven to 180°C/160°C fan/350°F/gas mark 4. Put the Jerusalem artichokes on a baking tray, drizzle with olive oil and a pinch of salt and put them in the oven. Ten minutes later, add the red onion tossed in a little olive oil. Roast for a further 15–20 minutes, until the artichokes have softened and are turning golden brown.

2. Remove from the oven and allow to cool slightly, before adding to the mixed leaves.

3. Combine the dressing ingredients with a pinch of sea salt and some black pepper, whisking to create an emulsion. Dress the salad and toss well, before crumbling the feta cheese over it.

LEEK AND SWEET POTATO FRITTATA

SERVES 2

1 small sweet potato, skin on,
   diced
2 small leeks, finely chopped
olive oil, for frying
4 large eggs
sea salt and pepper

MEDICINAL PROPERTIES
LEEKS SWEET POTATOES

This gorgeous dish makes a filling breakfast, or even a portable lunch, served with a side salad.

1. Put the sweet potato in a small saucepan and cover with boiling water. Simmer for about 15 minutes, or until the potato has softened, then drain. Alternatively, you could steam it.

2. In a small omelette pan, sauté the leeks in a little olive oil, along with a pinch of salt, until they soften. Add the sweet potato.

3. Crack the eggs into a bowl and whisk them, then add to the sweet potato and leek pan. Cook on a high heat, in a pan that will also be suitable for grilling, until the frittata is cooked around the edges. Place the pan under a hot grill until the top of the frittata is cooked. Check the centre by pricking with a knife. If runny egg sticks to the knife, return to the hob for a few minutes more, until the knife comes out clean.

4. Remove the frittata to a a plate and crack black pepper over the top.

TUMMY TEA

SERVES 1

2 tablespoons each of
  the following:
peppermint
bay leaf
fennel seeds
caraway seeds
dried liquorice root

This simple aromatic tea, drunk regularly, can strengthen digestive function. It will help to regulate peristaltic contractions, increase the production of digestive fluids, and reduce transit time, inflammation, bloating and gas.

1. Blend all the ingredients and store in an airtight jar as a loose tea to use daily (fresh peppermint and bay leaves will keep for 1-2 days; dried will keep for longer).

2. Use four teaspoons per cup. Put in a teapot or cafetière, cover with freshly boiled water and allow to brew for ten minutes.

MEDICINAL PROPERTIES

HERBS

DHAL SOUP

SERVES 2–3

1 large red onion, finely
  chopped
3 cloves of garlic, finely
  chopped
Olive oil, for frying
2 teaspoons turmeric
2 teaspoons garam masala
1 teaspoon cumin
375g red lentils
500ml vegetable stock
sea salt

This lovely simple soup is filling, nutrient dense,
and wonderful for overall digestive health.

1. Sauté the onion and garlic in a little olive oil, along
with a good pinch of sea salt, until the onion softens.

2. At this stage, add the turmeric, garam masala, and
cumin and keep stirring until the spices begin to stick
slightly to the bottom of the pan.

3. Add the lentils and the vegetable stock and simmer
for 40 minutes. If you find that the soup is too thick, then
top up the liquid with water to desired consistency.

MEDICINAL PROPERTIES

ONIONS AND GARLIC
RED LENTILS

GENERAL TIPS TO REMEMBER FOR DIGESTIVE HEALTH

BAY LEAVES have a 'carminative' effect that can ease gas and bloating. Like all the aromatic herbs mentioned here, the volatile oils in bay leaves give them their aromatic flavour.

FENNEL is another carminative. The aniseed-like oils help to relax the gut wall to ease bloating and gas.

GARLIC, like all the alliums, is a rich source of inulin, the prebiotic carbohydrate that works as a food source for gut flora, helping it to flourish.

GLOBE ARTICHOKES contain substances such as caffeoylquinic acid that have notable mild laxative effects. These aren't hardcore laxative effects, rather a gentle push.

JERUSALEM ARTICHOKES are another very rich source of prebiotic carbohydrates. In some cases they can cause a bit of bloating and gas. This is a temporary and necessary evil, and actually a sign that your gut flora is having a party.

MINT is the king of carminative herbs. The volatile oil menthol has been widely studied and is recognised as an effective carminative, helping to ease bloating and disperse gas and discomfort.

OATS are rich in a soluble fibre called beta glucan. This can help soften the stool and cause stretching of the gut wall, which in turn stimulates peristalsis.

PULSES such as lentils and beans have double benefit for digestive health. First, they have a very high fibre content. Second, many pulses have varying levels of prebiotic carbohydrates in them, helping to grow and nurture gut flora.

LEEKS, like all the onion family, are a great source of inulin, a potent prebiotic carbohydrate.

THE HEART AND CIRCULATORY SYSTEM

The circulatory system is our body's lifeline. Every tissue in our body requires a constant supply of oxygen and nutrients. Even seconds without such a supply would be life-threatening. This system comprises the heart, arteries, veins and capillaries. There are, in fact, two circulatory systems in the body. The first is our main systemic circulation that travels throughout the length and breadth of our body. The second is the pulmonary circulation. This is a loop-like system. When the blood delivers its oxygen to tissues, the deoxygenated blood returns to the lungs to receive a fresh load of oxygen from the air we breathe. The heart is the most sophisticated pumping system in existence, not matched by any technology. It beats 60–100 times per minute, 100,000 times a day, 30 million times per year and 2.5 billion times in a 70-year lifetime. That's pretty impressive!

Every day, the equivalent of more than 2,000 gallons of blood are pumped around the body. This staggering quantity flows through more than 60,000 miles of blood vessels, moving into every single tissue and structure within our body. Some are thick, wide arteries; some are blood vessels so thin and delicate that only a laboratory microscope can see them. This whole system is responsive to chemical messages that tell it how to perform in order to deliver more or less blood to different tissues, as their needs change.

Heart and circulatory disease is the biggest killer in the Western world – fact! In the UK alone, one in every four men and one in every six women will die from the condition, and more than 300,000 people will have a heart attack this year! There are many factors that contribute to this rather grim picture, but one of the biggest is our diet and lifestyle. The sequence of events and the way diet fits into the picture is discussed below (pages 71–75). First, we should familiarise ourselves with the structure and functions of the cardiovascular system. This way we can get a better understanding of how diet can be used therapeutically, and how indeed it can act to cause problems in the first place.

THE HEART

The central driving force of this whole sophisticated pumping system is the heart. This is a pump of such vast complexity that it could never be fully replicated by human hands. The pump takes blood that has given all its oxygen to our tissues and now flows back through our veins to our lungs, where it can become replete with oxygen again. The left- and right-hand sides of the heart each have a specific job to do. The right-hand side takes deoxygenated blood and sends it to the lungs to top it up with oxygen, and to remove carbon dioxide (that we then breathe out). The left-hand side takes blood that is freshly oxidised and pumps it out to the rest of the body.

THE BLOOD

The blood is an abundant liquid that is carried through our circulatory system and it is a very interesting and complex one at that. It is designed to carry oxygen and nutrients to our tissues – the oxygen from the air we breathe and the nutrients from the food we eat are all taken around the body by the blood. The blood also helps to carry away waste products from our cells and tissues for breakdown and removal. The blood is made up of several types of cell and structure that all have different roles to play.

Erythrocytes are the disc-shaped cells often seen in textbooks, otherwise known as red blood cells. Their primary job is to transport oxygen around the body, supplying it to our tissues. Our red blood cells contain a protein-based structure in them called haemoglobin. This is what is known as a metalloprotein, as it contains a metal as part of its structure. In the case of haemoglobin, the metal is iron. There are four irons bound to haemoglobin, and each one of these iron molecules binds to an oxygen molecule, so it can be transported. This is why low levels of iron can cause fatigue and low mood; our tissues don't receive the vital oxygen that they need to create energy and function properly.

Leukocytes are known more commonly as white blood cells. They are in essence the foot soldiers of our immune system. They can identify pathogens as they move through the body. They can also identify any cells and tissues that have become damaged or infected. They do this by reading signals on the surface of cells. This is covered in greater detail in the immune system chapter.

Thrombocytes are also sometimes referred to as platelets. Their role is to stop bleeding in injured areas. They flood the injured area and begin to plug the hole. When they form a plug, they begin to secrete chemical signals that stimulate the laying down of a fibrous structure called fibrin. This forms a protective netting around the plug to keep everything secure while the area has a chance to heal.

Plasma is the watery liquid that all the above cells are suspended in. It is mostly water, with various proteins and nutrients floating around in it.

alter its behaviour according to localised needs. The contraction and relaxation of this muscle is what controls our blood pressure.

The endothelium is the inner skin that lines our blood vessels. This isn't just passive barrier tissue. It is tissue that is highly physiologically active and maintains the function of the blood vessel. It produces a substance called nitric oxide – a gas that protects the endothelium from damage, but also, and most importantly, causes vasodilation. This is the relaxation of the smooth muscle described above, which makes the vessel widen and the pressure within it to drop.

BLOOD VESSELS

The blood vessels are a very intricate network that supply almost every inch of our body with blood. Some are as thick as a hosepipe, while others are thinner than a hair. Understanding how they work and the problems that can arise is key to understanding how nutrition can play a role in caring for the health of the heart. There are two important structural areas of the blood vessels to know about in this respect.

Smooth muscle is an involuntary muscle which makes up the walls of our blood vessels. This muscle is different from the skeletal muscle with which we voluntarily move. Smooth muscle responds to localised neurological and chemical messengers that

EATING FOR A HEALTHY HEART AND CARDIOVASCULAR SYSTEM

Many factors can affect heart health and our risk of heart disease. Smoking, excessive alcohol, stress, lack of exercise. These all play a role and must all be addressed. However, one of the biggest culprits in the increasing rise of heart disease is our dietary behaviour. On the flipside of this, changes in dietary habits can offer a high level of protection against cardiovascular disease. Let's not forget that the food we eat directly influences our physiology. There are a few key cardiovascular risk factors that can be notably influenced both positively and negatively by our diet.

REDUCE CHOLESTEROL

OK, so the debate about cholesterol continues. It does seem that high cholesterol may not be the risk factor it was once thought to be. However, this is still under debate, so for now, all I will say is that if you feel that lowering your cholesterol is something you want to do, or you are advised to do so by your doctor, then there are ways to do this through diet. Really, it mostly comes down to soluble fibre. There are two types of dietary fibre – soluble and insoluble. Both provide bulk to the contents of the digestive tract to keep everything moving along nicely. Insoluble fibre just takes on water and swells in size. Soluble fibre, however, is – as the name suggests – a soluble substance that becomes gel-like in the digestive tract. This can bind to cholesterol and carry it away before it is absorbed. This cholesterol isn't from food, it is cholesterol made by our liver. When cholesterol is made, a very high proportion of it is used in the manufacture of bile acids, which are released via the gall bladder for the digestion of fats. The small remainder goes straight into circulation to play a vital role in manufacturing hormones such as oestrogen or testosterone, and maintaining cell membrane structure and function. The cholesterol released into the upper digestive tract to carry out these digestive functions does its job, then moves lower into the digestive system for reabsorption, to join the rest of the cholesterol in its

vital duties. When we consume good sources of soluble fibre, the cholesterol that is on its way to join the rest in circulation will bind to the gel-like substance that forms, so it cannot be absorbed. Cholesterol is so vital for bile acid manufacture that if cholesterol isn't absorbed from the digestive tract, the body mobilises a proportion of what is in circulation to be put to that use. The end result is that serum cholesterol is reduced. Foods such as apples and oats are wonderful sources of soluble fibre.

SUPPORTING ENDOTHELIAL HEALTH AND FUNCTION

As mentioned previously, the endothelium (the inner skin that lines our blood vessels) is not a passive 'skin'. It is, in fact, very active physiologically and regulates a great deal of the health of the blood vessel. This is mostly through a chemical produced by the endothelial cells called nitric oxide. This substance helps to reduce excessive blood clotting and prevent cholesterol oxidation, which causes inflammatory damage to the endothelium. It is also the substance that controls the dilation of blood vessels.

In terms of diet, there are a group of compounds called flavonoids that have been widely studied, especially here in the UK. These compounds tend to be found in high concentrations in foods such as berries, red wine, green tea and chocolate. It has been found that flavonoids can be taken up by the endothelial cells and cause metabolic irritation, almost like a stress response within the cell. In response to this flavonoid-induced stress, the endothelial cells release higher concentrations of nitric oxide. This helps to protect the endothelium from inflammatory damage, but possibly most importantly from my point of view is that the increase in nitric oxide production will relax the smooth muscle tissue that makes up the main walls of the vessel. As these muscle fibres relax, the vessel dilates and widens. As the vessel widens, the pressure against the blood vessel walls reduces. So blood pressure is lowered. This is transient (i.e. it lasts for a limited period of time) but it highlights an important group of foods that anyone concerned with long-term heart health can regularly add to their diet to help lower blood pressure.

REDUCING INFLAMMATION

Heart disease is essentially an inflammatory condition. Before anything else happens – before cholesterol gets involved, before plaques form – inflammation causes damage to the endothelium. Factors such as oxidised cholesterol and excessive blood sugar levels, and the wrong types of fat in the diet, can cause microscopic inflammatory damage to the endothelium. When such damage occurs, circulating materials such as cholesterol that rush through the vessels can begin to be forced into the area of damage, penetrating the vessel walls and embedding themselves within, triggering further inflammation. At this point, the immune system gets involved and certain cell lines start to follow this debris into the vessel walls and engulf this material. When they do this, they stay put and turn into something called a 'foam cell'. This is the first stage in the formation of a plaque or a fatty streak. This fatty streak can be surrounded by muscle cells and structures such as fibrin, and the plaque becomes fairly stable – almost like a semi-repaired injury site. This can stay stable for years, but if we continue to follow a poor diet, smoke too much, drink too much and take no exercise, we run the risk of rupturing these sites of injury (not to mention creating new ones). When these sites rupture, the ruptured bleeding plaque will cause a clot. This clot can then easily be knocked or broken up by the force of circulating blood if the clot or a piece of it should break off and travel through the circulatory system.

As the circulatory system extends out further and further, vessels become smaller and smaller. Sooner or later the clot will reach a vessel too small to accommodate it. When this happens, the clot blocks the vessel, which cuts off the blood supply to whichever tissue is supplied by the blocked vessel. This cuts off the oxygen supply to the tissue, and the tissue can die. This is called an infarction. When it happens to a vessel that supplies the heart, it is a heart attack and when it happens in a vessel that supplies the brain, a stroke. So, while plaques and the clot formation that follows their rupture are the more obviously deadly part of the picture, the inflammation that caused all the damage in the first place is the initial trigger. Manage inflammation – and reduce your risk of heart disease!

So, how do we manage inflammation with diet? The easiest way is to be aware of the types of fats that we consume. The fats in our diet contain substances called fatty acids. These are vitamin-like substances found in fats that provide our body with the building blocks it needs to manufacture key structural compounds such as cell membranes, as well as communication compounds that control specific biochemical events in the body. An example of this is a group of compounds called prostaglandins. These regulate several things in the body, but the main one is the inflammatory response. There are three key prostaglandins – series 1, series 2 and series 3. Series 1 and 3 prostaglandins switch off and reduce inflammation. Series 2 prostaglandins, on the other hand, switch on and exacerbate inflammation. Different fatty acids, found in different types of fats in the diet, are metabolised to form different types of prostaglandins. So, already you can see that the different types of fats in your diet supply different fatty acids, which will metabolise into different prostaglandins. If you happen to be eating the types of fats that are rich in the type of fatty acids that metabolise into the pro-inflammatory series 2 prostaglandins, you will in essence be throwing

petrol on the bonfire! But load your diet with the fats that are rich in fatty acids that metabolise into series 1 and 3 prostaglandins, and you will increase the production of the substances that reduce inflammation.

What does this look like in practice? If you consume oils such as vegetable oil, sunflower oil, corn oil, soya bean oil and vegetable margarine, then you are consuming high levels of a fatty acid called omega 6. This is one of the fatty acids that get converted into the pro-inflammatory series 2 prostaglandins. Consume these products daily, and you fan the inflammatory flame big time! This can cause inflammatory damage all over the body, not just in the cardiovascular system. Consuming oils such as those found in oily fish such as salmon, mackerel, herrings or fresh tuna will provide you with the omega 3 fatty acids EPA and DHA that metabolise to form the anti-inflammatory series 1 and series 3 prostaglandins.

So the key to putting this into practice from day to day is very simple: stop using vegetable oils and switch to olive oil and occasionally coconut oil (these don't contain significant enough levels of omega 6 fatty acids to cause a problem). Also, stop using vegetable margarine and swap to butter. The second step is to increase your intake of omega 3 fatty acids from marine sources such as the oily fish mentioned previously, or take a supplement. I should clarify here the claim that many people make that seeds such as flax and chia are a good source of omega 3. They are not. They contain loads of omega 3, but in a form called ALA. This has to be converted by a series of enzymes to form EPA and DHA – the types that feed into the metabolic pathways that manufacture series 1 and series 3 prostaglandins. Human beings only convert around six per cent of dietary ALA into EPA and DHA, so you would need to eat kilos and kilos of seeds every day to even get a sniff at the kind of levels of EPA and DHA you need daily.

KEY FOODS FOR HEART HEALTH

APPLES

Apples are rich in a source of soluble fibre called pectin, which can help to reduce cholesterol from the digestive tract.

FLAX SEEDS

These seeds don't have any value as a source of omega 3, but they are a great addition to a heart-healthy diet as they have a good level of soluble fibre to help reduce cholesterol.

GARLIC

Rich in a substance called ajoene, garlic influences clotting factors and can reduce excessive clotting and clot formation.

OATS

Oats have been clinically proven to lower cholesterol because they contain a soluble fibre called beta glucan. This forms a gel-like substance in the digestive tract which binds to cholesterol and carries it away before it can be absorbed.

OILY FISH

Fish such as salmon and mackerel are great sources of the vital omega 3 fatty acids EPA and DHA, which are metabolised to form the powerfully anti-inflammatory series 1 and series 3 prostaglandins, and also resolvins, helping to protect the endothelium from inflammatory damage.

RED ONIONS

Red onions, along with other purple foods, such as blackberries, are packed with a group of phytochemicals called flavonoids. These are taken up by endothelial cells, increasing nitric oxide release. This helps to protect the endo-thelium from damage, and also dilates the blood vessel to help reduce the pressure within it.

RECIPES FOR HEART HEALTH
– TOP INGREDIENTS –

The recipes that follow contain ingredients which have medicinal properties that benefit the heart and circulatory system. Here is a rundown of these star ingredients and their medicinal properties:

APPLES (pages 90 and 95) have long been renowned for keeping the doctor away. They contain a type of soluble fibre known as pectin. You may have come across pectin if you are a fan of making your own jams. It is used as a natural gelling agent. Pectin, just like beta glucan, binds to cholesterol and carries it out of the body via the bowel. The story doesn't end there, however. There is also a group of chemicals in apples called polyphenols. These are believed to lower LDL cholesterol, possibly by influencing the production of HDL over LDL. The final magic ingredient in apples is a substance called ellagic acid. This helps to break down excessive cholesterol in the liver and also protects cells from damage, which has to be good.

AVOCADOS (page 96) are a very rich source of oleic acid, which has notable effects upon lowering cholesterol. Avocados are also a very rich source of vitamin E, which can help to protect against excessive blood clotting, and also helps to reduce chemical damage to fats that are circulating in our blood. Chemical damage to these fats can cause injury to blood vessel walls and increase the likelihood of clot formation.

BEETROOT (page 88) is a great source of nitrates. When consumed, these are converted into nitric oxide. This is a substance that is naturally produced by the endothelium – the highly active skin that lines the inner surface of our blood vessels. Nitric oxide relaxes the smooth muscle walls of the blood vessels. When they relax, the vessels dilate and the pressure within them drops. So eating beetroot can temporarily lower blood pressure and improve blood flow.

BUTTERNUT SQUASH (page 86) is packed with beta-carotene, the compound that gives it its lovely orange colour. This antioxidant can help to reduce cholesterol oxidation and also reduces inflammation at a local level.

CACAO (page 96), or raw chocolate, is awash with more than 1,500 active chemicals that can have an amazing impact upon our health. In the context of heart health, though, raw chocolate has two major benefits. First, it is an incredibly dense source of the vital mineral magnesium. Magnesium is involved in regulating gut mobility and heart rhythm. It is also used alongside calcium in maintaining and regulating muscular relaxation and contraction. (Calcium causes muscle fibres to contract, whereas magnesium makes them relax.) The walls of the blood vessels are made up of many layers of muscle. Increasing our intake of magnesium can play a role in maintaining a healthy blood pressure. The second major benefit of cacao is its incredibly high antioxidant content. Although chocolate appears brown, it is in fact a very deep purple colour. This is because of an incredibly dense concentration of plant pigments that deliver powerful antioxidant benefits, useful because it helps to protect blood vessels from damage and reduce the oxidization of cholesterol.

CHICKPEAS (page 89) contain a chemical cocktail that is beneficial to heart health, including saponins, lignans and phytos-

terols. The best understood of the bunch are the phytosterols. These are the compound found in myriad cholesterol-lowering spreads and drinks. They help to lower cholesterol by binding to it and carrying it out of the body via the bowel. They are also a rich source of magnesium, which can help to lower blood pressure and regulate heart rhythm.

FETA CHEESE (page 86) is not only great taste wise, it plays a role too. Beta-carotene is a fat-soluble antioxidant. The fats in feta cheese increase the absorption of beta-carotene many times, helping to get the most out of foods rich in it. Whenever you eat carotenoid-rich foods, add some fats.

FLAX SEEDS (page 83) are high in a soluble fibre similar to oats that can bind to cholesterol. The cholesterol is therefore carried away via the bowel before it gets a chance to be absorbed. The long term effect of this is a lowering of serum cholesterol.

GARLIC (pages 85, 89, 90, 93, 94) contains a powerful antioxidant that is believed to prevent LDL ('bad') cholesterol from oxidising. This is the process that causes cholesterol to clog up arteries, so anything we can do to stop this has to be a winner. Garlic also contains sulphurous chemicals that are believed to affect the production of this 'bad' cholesterol transporter, thus leading to a greater presence of the 'good' HDL. Garlic also contains a potent compound called ajoene. This chemical interacts with a biochemical messenger called platelet-aggregating factor. This compound tells the platelets in the blood to stick together and form a blood clot. The ajoene found in fresh garlic helps to lower heart attack risk in general, although we must note that this protective effect comes from prolonged use.

MACKEREL (page 90) is packed with omega 3 fatty acids, possibly one of the most important nutrient groups for cardio-vascular health. These fatty substances have been shown to improve LDL to HDL cholesterol ratios. Most importantly, though, they are anti-inflammatory. They are the metabolic building blocks that the body uses to manufacture its own inherent anti-inflammatory compounds called prostaglandins. By consuming high levels of omega 3, we force-feed the production of these anti-inflammatory compounds. Inflammatory damage to the inner lining of the blood vessels is the instigating factor in the sequence of events that causes heart disease.

NUTS (pages 93, 96) are packed with many amazing compounds and nutrients. They are a very rich source of the mineral selenium. This vital nutrient is used by the body to make its own natural anti-inflammatory enzymes, mainly SOD (superoxide dismutase). This enzyme is also believed to be a part of the body's natural protection mechanisms against damage to arterial walls. Many nuts have been shown to have significant LDL cholesterol-lowering properties. This may be due to the fact that many nuts are high in the compound oleic acid. This is the same chemical that is found in olive oil, and is responsible for olive oil's cardio-protective properties.

OATS (pages 83, 84, 95) contain a soluble fibre called beta glucan. This has been studied extensively and is clinically proven to lower cholesterol. It does this by forming a gel-like substance in the digestive tract. This binds to cholesterol that has entered the digestive tract from the liver via the bile. Normally it would be reabsorbed. Beta glucan binds to it and prevents it from being reabsorbed. This can lower serum cholesterol.

ONIONS (pages 86, 88, 94) have a million and one medicinal applications, but have been shown in clinical trials to be especially beneficial to the health of the heart and circulatory system. They contain a group of compounds called sterols. These are the same plant chemicals that are added to spreads and drinks designed to lower cholesterol. Sterols help to reduce the uptake of cholesterol through the gut wall. This can be cholesterol from foods, or cholesterol that has been made in the liver and released via the gall bladder into the digestive tract. Onions also contain a group of sulphur-type compounds that can help to reduce clotting in the blood, so offer a protective role against heart attacks and strokes. Red onions have another protective substance: the purple pigment that gives them their distinctive colour, which comes from a group of pigment chemicals called flavonoids. These help to protect the inner lining of the blood vessels from damage.

ORANGES (page 96) contain a group of compounds called bioflavonoids. These are found in the rind and pith of the orange, and are known to protect the inner lining of blood vessels from damage. They do this by strengthening the microscopic mesh that holds all the cells together within the lining. This mesh is found in every solid body tissue and is known as the 'extracellular matrix'.

PEARL BARLEY (page 90) is rich in soluble fibre and insoluble fibre. These are vital in maintaining cardiovascular health. This is because they bind to cholesterol in the digestive tract, and carry it away before it can be absorbed. This is cholesterol that has been produced by our liver, leached into the digestive tract with bile during fat digestion.

PEARS (page 84) have a similar fibre content to oats, so enhance cholesterol-lowering properties.

PUY LENTILS (page 88) are similar to grains such as oats, and contain soluble fibre that can bind to cholesterol within the digestive tract.

RED PEPPERS (pages 93, 94) contain the vivid colour pigment chemicals called flavonoids, mentioned above. These compounds are responsible for the red colour of the peppers. They are powerful antioxidant agents that, according to the *American Journal of Clinical Nutrition*, play a significant role in the prevention of atherosclerosis. Flavonoids are also notable anti-inflammatory agents, so with the new information linking inflammation and heart disease, adding anti-inflammatory foods to your daily diet is an absolute must.

SHIITAKE MUSHROOMS (page 85) are amazing Asian treasures that have long been known as a powerful stimulant to the immune system, and are commonly used in flu-fighting potions and soups. However, many recent clinical trials in China and Japan have shown that shiitake may offer protection against high cholesterol. This is due to the presence of a compound called eritadenine. Eritadenine appears to encourage the conversion of the 'bad' LDL cholesterol into the 'good' HDL cholesterol, and also generally lower blood lipids (fats).

SUNFLOWER SEEDS (page 85) are a fantastically rich source of a group of plant chemicals called phytosterols. These are the chemicals made famous by the myriad cholesterol-lowering drinks, yoghurts and spreads on the market. They help to reduce the level of cholesterol taken up by the digestive tract. Cholesterol moves around the body in a bit of a loop system. It is made in the liver from specific dietary fats and then transported throughout the body via several mechanisms. One mechanism in particular involves cholesterol being released from the liver into the digestive tract, where it is reabsorbed into the general circulation. Phytosterols actually block this reabsorption, thus allowing the cholesterol in the gut to be removed from the body via the bowel. The cholesterol-lowering activities of phytosterols have been very well documented in recent years, adding to their popularity.

TURMERIC (page 89) is a well known anticoagulant (preventer of clotting), and is also a potent anti-inflammatory. The yellow pigment in turmeric helps to control inflammation, so can give significant protection against inflammatory damage of the inner lining of the blood vessels.

CINNAMON FLAX GRANOLA

MAKES 6–8 PORTIONS

2 tablespoons olive oil
125ml maple syrup
1 teaspoon vanilla extract
1 teaspoon cinnamon
300g rolled oats (not
  porridge oats)
50g flax seeds
50g pumpkin seeds
100g flaked almonds

MEDICINAL PROPERTIES

FLAX SEEDS
OATS

I'm not a huge fan of cereals for breakfast, as many of them are packed full of all sorts of rubbish. Making your own, however, means you can control what goes into it.

1. Preheat the oven to 150°C/130°C fan/300°F/gas mark 2. Mix the oil, maple syrup, vanilla extract and cinnamon together in a bowl. Add the remaining ingredients and toss well to ensure that everything is covered in the wet ingredients.

2. Spread the granola on baking sheets. You may need two or three sheets. It is important that the granola covers each sheet in a single thin layer.

3. Bake for about 30 minutes. Keep your eye on it as ovens vary. You want it to turn crisp and golden brown. Store in an airtight container and serve with yoghurt, topped with a fruit of your choice.

COCONUT PORRIDGE WITH
SPICED ROASTED PEAR PURÉE

SERVES 2

1 large ripe pear, skin on,
    cut into wedges, seeds
    removed
½ teaspoon mixed spice
80g porridge oats
400ml coconut milk

MEDICINAL PROPERTIES

OATS
PEARS

This fibre-packed creamy breakfast is the perfect
heart-healthy start on a cold morning.

1. Preheat the oven to 180°C/160°C fan/350°F/gas mark 4.
Put the pear wedges on a baking tray and bake for
about 20 minutes until they are soft and beginning
to caramelise.

2. Put the roasted pears into a food processor with the
mixed spice. Blend into a coarse purée. Add a little
water if needed.

3. Put the oats and coconut milk in a saucepan and bring
to a simmer. The porridge will thicken quite quickly, so
feel free to add a little water if you want a thinner texture.

SHIITAKE SUNFLOWER SPREAD

SERVES 2

150g punnet fresh shiitake
  mushrooms
3 tablespoons raw sunflower
  seeds
2 cloves garlic
3 tablespoons extra virgin
  olive oil
dash soy sauce
sea salt and pepper

A gorgeous smooth, mushroomy pâté that is divine spread on crackers, toast or as a dip for veggies. Its deep, earthy flavour keeps people coming back for more.

This is the easiest dip in the world to make. Just throw all the ingredients into a food processor and blend them into a smooth dip. That's it! No, really, that's actually it. Season to taste. You can add more oil if you prefer a slightly thinner dip.

MEDICINAL PROPERTIES

GARLIC
SHIITAKE MUSHROOMS
SUNFLOWER SEEDS

ROASTED RED ONION, SQUASH AND FETA SALAD

SERVES 2

¼ butternut squash, skin on,
   cut into bite-size pieces
1 large red onion, cut into
   wedges
olive oil to drizzle
2 handfuls mixed leaves
80g feta cheese
sea salt

for the dressing
1 tablespoon olive oil
1 teaspoon apple cider
   vinegar
¼ teaspoon garlic granules

This super simple salad is just gorgeous. Packed with heart-healthy nutrients, and very simple to make. It is great as a side dish with a summer barbecue or even as a main dish.

1. Preheat the oven to 180°C/fan 160°C/350°F/gas mark 4. Put the squash and onion wedges on a roasting tray. Drizzle with a little olive oil, add a pinch of sea salt and toss well. Roast for 25–30 minutes, until both are soft and turning golden brown on some edges.

2. Combine the roasted squash, onion and mixed leaves. Crumble over the feta cheese.

3. Mix all the dressing ingredients and whisk thoroughly to ensure that the vinegar and oil combine. Dress the salad and toss well.

MEDICINAL PROPERTIES

BUTTERNUT SQUASH
FETA CHEESE
ONIONS

ROASTED BEETROOT, CARAMELISED RED ONION, PUY LENTIL AND GOAT'S CHEESE WARM SALAD

SERVES 2

2 medium raw beetroot, scrubbed, cut into wedges
olive oil, for drizzling and frying
1 large red onion, halved, then sliced
1 teaspoon honey
250g cooked puy lentils
100g soft goat's cheese
small bunch curly parsley, roughly chopped
sea salt and pepper

This is a great main course salad that is light but will keep you going for hours.

1. Preheat the oven to 180°C/160°C fan/350°F/gas mark 4. Put the beetroot wedges on a baking sheet, drizzle with olive oil and roast for about 35–40 minutes until soft.

2. In a frying pan, sauté the onion in a little olive oil until soft. Add the honey and continue to cook until caramelised.

3. Mix the roasted beetroot with the lentils. Add the onions and toss well.

4. Crumble over the goats' cheese, add the parsley and a pinch of salt and pepper, then lightly toss again.

MEDICINAL PROPERTIES

BEETROOT
PUY LENTILS
RED ONIONS

SPICY CHICKPEAS

SERVES 2

2–3 tablespoons olive or
   coconut oil
2 cloves garlic, finely chopped
2.5cm piece ginger, peeled
   and finely chopped
1 fresh green chilli, chopped
400g can chickpeas, drained
½ teaspoon ground cumin
½ teaspoon ground coriander
½ teaspoon ground turmeric
½ teaspoon garam masala
½ teaspoon ground cinnamon
sea salt or Himalayan
   crystal salt

I love this dish. It is a simple, easy and incredibly tasty side dish that has many benefits for a healthy heart and cardiovascular system.

1. Heat the olive oil or coconut oil in a saucepan over a high heat. Add the garlic, and allow it to brown to give it a smoky flavour.

2. Add a couple of pinches of salt, then the ginger and chilli, and allow to cook for a minute or two, until the ginger begins to get more fragrant.

3. Add the chickpeas and mix thoroughly. Add all the ground spices apart from the cinnamon. Mix thoroughly again, and allow to simmer for about two minutes. Take the pan off the heat and stir in the cinnamon.

MEDICINAL PROPERTIES

CHICKPEAS
GARLIC
TURMERIC

PAN-FRIED MACKEREL WITH SLOW-COOKED BARLEY AND RED CABBAGE SLAW

SERVES 2

1 white onion, finely chopped
2 cloves garlic, finely chopped
olive oil, for frying
125g pearl barley
400ml hot vegetable stock
80g red cabbage, very thinly
   sliced
¼ small red onion, very thinly
   sliced
¼ red apple, skin on, finely
   grated
2 tsp mayonnaise
½ teaspoon wasabi
2 mackerel fillets
sea salt and pepper

MEDICINAL PROPERTIES

APPLES
GARLIC
MACKEREL
PEARL BARLEY

This is a lovely filling dish that is nutrient dense, keeps you feeling full for hours and has multiple heart health benefits.

1. Begin by sautéeing the white onion and garlic in a saucepan in a little olive oil, along with a pinch of salt, until the onion has softened.

2. Add the pearl barley and a small amount of stock. Treat this dish like a risotto, and add small amounts of stock little and often, stirring frequently. Keep this up until the barley is soft and has a creamy risotto-like texture. If you run out of stock, you can use a little water (adding more stock may make the risotto too salty). Once cooked, set aside.

3. Put the cabbage, onion, apple, mayonnaise and wasabi in a bowl with a pinch of salt and some pepper, and mix well.

4. Pan-fry the mackerel for 5–8 minutes, turning occasionally.

5. Place a generous helping of the barley in the centre of two serving plates, top each with a mackerel fillet, then place a good spoonful of the slaw on top of the mackerel.

SPINACH-STUFFED CHICKEN WITH RED PEPPER PESTO, WHITE BEANS AND CITRUS WATERCRESS

SERVES 2

3 handfuls baby spinach
olive oil, for frying
2 skinless chicken breasts
400g can cannellini beans, drained
400g can butter beans, drained
2 handfuls watercress

for the pesto
2 red peppers, halved and deseeded
1 clove garlic, roughly chopped
2 tablespoons pine nuts
2 tablespoons raw cashew nuts
5g basil leaves
2 tablespoons olive oil
sea salt

for the citrus dressing
juice of half a clementine
1 teaspoon lemon juice
1 tablespoon extra virgin olive oil
salt and pepper

MEDICINAL PROPERTIES

GARLIC
NUTS
RED PEPPERS

A comforting, succulent dinner with delicious red pepper pesto.

1. Preheat the oven to 180°C/160°C fan/350°F/gas mark 4. Put the peppers on a roasting tray and roast for 15–20 minutes. They need to be softened and turning black on the skins.

2. Put the peppers, garlic, pine nuts, cashews, basil, olive oil and a good pinch of salt into a food processor and blitz into a coarse pesto.

3. Gently sauté the spinach in a tiny bit of olive oil until it has wilted.

4. Cut a slit in the side of each chicken breast to create a pocket. Stuff the pockets with the spinach, and seal and secure them with a cocktail stick. Place the stuffed chicken breasts on a roasting tray and roast for about 25–30 minutes.

5. Put the beans and pesto in a saucepan, mix well, then warm through over a low heat.

6. Combine all the dressing ingredients and whisk well. Dress the watercress leaves.

7. Carve the chicken into 2cm thick slices so as to expose the spinach filling. Place on top of a serving of the pesto beans, and then garnish the plate with the dressed watercress.

RED RATATOUILLE AND BULGAR WHEAT STACK

SERVES 4

2 handfuls dry bulgar wheat
1 teaspoon vegetable stock
  powder
3 tablespoons olive oil
1 red onion, finely chopped
2 cloves garlic, finely chopped
10 vine-ripened cherry
  tomatoes, chopped
1 red pepper, deseeded and
  chopped
side salad, to serve
sea salt

MEDICINAL PROPERTIES

GARLIC
ONIONS
RED PEPPERS

This dish looks fabulous, is light and packed with some exciting plant chemicals that are known to be beneficial in the reduction of LDL cholesterol.

1. Put the dried bulgar wheat in a saucepan and cover it with water. Add the stock powder and bring to the boil.

2. In another saucepan, add the olive oil, onion and garlic. Add a pinch of salt and sauté until the onion and garlic are soft.

3. Add the tomatoes and red pepper, and cook until the pepper has softened and the tomatoes have broken down to become a thick sauce.

4. On a serving plate, place a layer of the tomato and pepper mixture into a cooking ring mould or deep round cookie cutter. Pack the mixture in tightly to around the halfway mark. Then put a layer of bulgar wheat on top, all the way to the top of the mould. Carefully remove the mould to reveal a two-layer stack.

5. Serve with a good dense side salad.

APPLE JACKS

MAKES 6–10

2 fresh apples, skin on
3 tablespoons dark agave
  nectar
5 tablespoons walnut oil
180g porridge oats
25g chopped dates
2 teaspoons cinnamon

MEDICINAL PROPERTIES
APPLES
OATS

Isn't it nice to have the occasional sweet treat? And why shouldn't we? We should be able to have small moments of decadence, and still be doing our health some good. Lovely, light, sweet, delicious apple flapjacks. One bite just won't be enough of these. A sweet treat that's great for you – does life get much better?

1. Preheat the oven to 180°C/160°C fan/350°F/gas mark 4.

2. Purée the apples in a food processor.

3. Put the agave nectar and walnut oil in a saucepan, and place on a medium heat. Mix the two thoroughly.

4. Add the oats and dates to the oil and agave nectar, and mix until the oats are moist.

5. Stir in the apple purée and mix thoroughly.

6. Press the mixture into a greased baking tin and bake for about 25–30 minutes.

7. Sprinkle the cinnamon on top, cut into squares and devour.

CHOCOLATE ORANGE TRUFFLE TORTE

SERVES 4–6

for the base
200g raw mixed nuts
30g melted raw cacao butter
2 tablespoons agave nectar

for the filling
2 soft, ripe Hass avocados
zest and juice of 1 large
    orange
2 tablespoons agave nectar
50g raw cashew nuts
3 heaped tablespoons raw
    cacao powder
30g melted raw cacao butter

MEDICINAL PROPERTIES

AVOCADOS
CACAO
NUTS
ORANGES

No, your eyes aren't deceiving you, and, yes, you are still reading the same book! I created this dish to prove that healthy food can also be a decadent, delicious and delightful affair. Why should we feel we are missing out on something because we choose to eat healthily? This recipe is just as delicious as a gourmet restaurant equivalent. I have even given it to people without telling them what it was made from, and they thought I'd finally cracked and given in to some naughty treats – they nearly fell off their chairs when I told them what went into it!

1. To make the base, put the nuts in a blender and blend into a coarse powder.

2. Melt the cacao butter in a glass bowl over a saucepan of water on a medium heat. Add to the blended nuts along with the agave nectar, and mix thoroughly.

3. Press the mixture into a flan tin, or cheesecake tin, as if you were making a cheesecake base. Allow the crust to go up the sides, so it looks similar to a flan case. Place the lined tin in the freezer for at least half an hour to allow the cacao butter to set rapidly.

4. Meanwhile, make the filling by scooping the avocado flesh into a food processor, along with the orange zest and juice.Add the agave nectar, cashew nuts and the cacao powder, and blend until a smooth, rich, chocolate pudding-like texture is reached.

5. Melt the second batch of cacao butter in the same way as the first and add to the other ingredients, then process on a lower setting until the butter is evenly mixed.

6. Remove the tin from the freezer, and scoop the chocolatey filling into the semi-set base. Spread out evenly, and then place in the refrigerator for 4 hours. The base will set to a biscuity texture, and the filling will become firm, like chocolate mousse. One taste of this and you will feel that all your birthdays have come at once!

GENERAL TIPS TO REMEMBER FOR HEART HEALTH

While there is an abundance of individual ingredients that can have a powerful influence upon specific factors of heart health, some changes in diet and lifestyle can have a drastic effect on the health of the heart and circulatory system. The good news is that they are easy to adopt. Heart disease is fortunately incredibly responsive to changes in diet and lifestyle. Even the smallest changes can have a massive impact on our risk of heart disease, not to mention a drastic improvement in any damage or issues that may already be present.

REDUCE SATURATED FAT INTAKE. The first dietary change to make is reducing your saturated fat intake. This means cutting back on foods such as red meat, hard cheeses, milk and cream. All dietary fats influence the manufacture of certain products in our bodies. These could be the production of communication molecules called prostaglandins that regulate the inflammatory response and pain signalling. They also determine which types of cholesterol/lipoprotein complexes are formed. Saturated fat encourages the production of LDL, the 'bad' cholesterol carrier, which, in the long term, can lead to fatty deposits on the artery walls. By changing the type of fats we consume, we can alter the levels of the 'good' and 'bad' cholesterol carriers.

However, I would also advise everyone to give up vegetable spreads tomorrow. No, actually, do it now! There have been huge mass-marketing campaigns which attempt to persuade us to give up butter in favour of margarine, in order to protect us against the dreaded dangers of saturated fat. All I said above is most certainly true. However, there is an abundance of new evidence that suggests that the margarine spreads are drastically worse for us than saturated fat could ever be. This is because they contain hydrogenated fats. Vegetable oils are naturally liquid at room temperature. To get them to look and behave in the same way as butter, manufacturers have to bubble hydrogen gas through the oil. This changes the chemical structure of the fat, and turns it into a semi-solid spread. The change in chemical structure creates something that the body finds impossible to recognise and deal with once we consume it. New data coming into the spotlight in recent years suggests that the consumption of such spreads is worse than butter. What do I recommend? I'd use butter every time. The body knows what it is, and how to deal with it. Just be sensible about how much you use.

PLANT-FOCUSED DIET. The second, and probably single most important, tip for a heart-healthy diet is to drastically increase your intake of fruit and vegetables, with the emphasis being on the veggies. Fresh plant foods are abundant in vitamins, minerals and antioxidants, which are all pivotal to the general health of our body. Antioxidants, in particular, can help to reduce damage to tissues such as blood vessel walls.

However, the nutrients in fresh plant foods are just the beginning of the story. Fresh plant foods contain a whole cocktail of active chemicals that aren't nutrients, but are very powerful medicinal compounds. These foods are also naturally low in fat, and fill you up for longer.

INCREASE HIGH-FIBRE FOODS. The third diet tip is to up your intake of high-fibre foods, such as wholegrains and pulses. These foods contain high levels of both

soluble and insoluble fibre, which can help to bind to cholesterol and carry it out of the body. These foods also make you feel fuller faster, so can be great weight-loss tools too.

THE IMMUNE SYSTEM

The body is a truly wondrous creation – such levels of complexity, organisation and communication. It seems strange to think that such an incredibly complex creation could be completely destroyed by a tiny bacteria. The smallest pathogen could mean the end of us. To protect us against this we have one of the most complex, multi-layered defence systems imaginable. Our immunity, being a biological system, of course requires specific nutrients in specific amounts, and responds rapidly to changes in the internal biochemical terrain. So we can influence our immune function through diet.

This is the shortest of all the modules, but one of the most important. Understanding the simple nutritional tweaks that can be made to support immunity will stand you in extremely good stead.

ORGANISATION OF THE IMMUNE SYSTEM

The immune system isn't just one thing in one place. There are many facets to this complex system, and many elements that protect our body from opportunistic pathogens and damaging infectious agents. Each aspect of immunity will offer different types and different levels of protection.

PHYSICAL BARRIERS

Physical barriers are the first level of immunological protection. The first and most obvious of these is, of course, our skin. Very few pathogens can penetrate our intact skin. They rely on cuts and wounds to penetrate the body. This is why cuts heal so rapidly. The structural integrity of the skin needs to

remain intact. As well as being a physical barrier, our skin has other means of warding off pathogens. The surface of the skin is rather acidic. This acidity makes it an unfavourable surface for many pathogens. The skin's surface is also home to a vast bacterial colony that lives symbiotically with us. These bacteria are rather protective of their homes and initiate aggressive responses to other bacteria and pathogens that may compete with them.

Our skin covers only about two square metres of the body, but a much greater surface area needs the protection of a physical barrier. Inside the body, many organs and tissues are protected by mucous membranes. These too are a type of skin, but have a secretory function. They not only supply the physical barrier of a skin, but the mucus they secrete offers a further level of protection.

THE INNATE IMMUNE SYSTEM

This is the second level of immunity. It is the first aspect of immunity that kicks in when a pathogen of some sort penetrates the physical barrier. It is called our innate immunity because we are born with it fully functioning, ready to operate when needed, unlike other aspects of the immune system that develop over time, as you will see a little later. Within our tissues are several types of white blood cell that circulate around the body looking for any foreign invader or damaged tissue. One of the main types of cell within the innate immune system is the macrophage. These large white cells engulf pathogens and send chemical signals to other circulating immune cells, to localised circulation and to nerve endings. This will be discussed in greater detail when I look at each different blood cell in turn. There are also cells, such as natural killer cells, and toxic biochemical compounds that form part of innate immunity too, but again, this will all begin to come clear when we get up close and personal with the different cells of the immune system.

ADAPTIVE/LEARNED IMMUNITY

This is the third stage of immunity, and one that is unique to only a handful of species of animal on the planet. Most animals seem to cope just fine with innate immunity. Human beings have developed this third powerful arm of the immune system, for reasons unknown. Adaptive immunity is the type of immunity that is antibody mediated. This means that the immune system, once challenged by a specific pathogen, learns the correct way in which to respond to it in future. This branch of the immune system is able to manufacture specific specialised proteins which circulate, and are able to tell the immune system what to do, should the body be invaded by the same pathogen in the future.

THE CELLS OF THE IMMUNE SYSTEM

Now I have outlined the three main ways in which the immune system is organised, it is time to get familiar with the cells that make up the immune system and their functions. This will give you greater detail about innate and adaptive immunity.

MACROPHAGES

Macrophages are very large white blood cells whose primary role is eating (macrophage means 'large eater'). They are found in high numbers in our tissues, where most of the time they are in a resting state, milling around, swallowing up general junk and waste, such as metabolic by-products and waste materials that have been kicked out of cells. If our first line of defence – the physical barriers – is breached, for example if we get a cut or a splinter, then macrophages begin to receive a variety of chemical signals. This chemical cascade alerts the macrophage and changes it from a resting state to an active state.

Once activated, the macrophage continues its eating habits, but to a much more aggressive extent. They approach invading pathogens and begin to elongate themselves. Rather than waiting until they bump into the pathogen, they stretch themselves out to reach it as soon as possible. Once they reach it, they begin to engulf and surround it, forming a pouch called a vesicle. This pouch is drawn inside the macrophage, where it floats around like a little bubble containing the pathogen. Inside the macrophages are other bubble-like things called lysosomes. These bubbles are filled with extremely potent chemicals and enzymes that can completely destroy bacteria. The lysosome binds with the vesicle, exposing the bacteria to the toxic substances, destroying them completely. Once the bacteria have been destroyed, the remnants are spat out for removal. This isn't the only way that macrophages help with our immunity. They also can deliver messages to other cells of the immune system. When they become activated, they display something called 'major histocompatability complex class II' (MHC II for short) on their outer surface. They incorporate fragments of proteins from the invader into the MHC II and display them to cells called T helper cells. Once the T helper cells have seen this signal, they can instigate further relevant immunological reactions such as localised inflammation.

NEUTROPHILS

Neutrophils are the most abundant white blood cell in the body. They represent up to 70 per cent of the entire white cell population of the body, and we produce up to 100 billion of these cells per day! They are also a phagocytic cell (meaning they engulf things in the same way as a macrophage does). They do not act as antigen-presenting cells as macrophages can (remember how macrophages display MHC to other cells of the immune system); they are purely professional eating machines. These potent cells don't just eat and destroy willy-nilly, they move through our circulation in a resting state. They become activated only when they leave the circulation.

The way they are activated is truly fascinating. They move through the vessels in our circulation at an incredibly high speed. When macrophages make the first contact with a pathogen, as we have seen, one of their responses is to secrete a group of compounds called cytokines – chemical messengers. When relevant cytokines are secreted by macrophages, they stimulate the production of a protein called selectin. This protein is then shuttled to the endothelium – the inner lining of the blood vessels that we covered in great detail in the heart module. When this protein is displayed on the endothelium, it binds to an adhesion molecule on the surface of neutrophils, called selectin ligand. When the binding takes place, it works a bit like Velcro. The neutrophils stick to this protein, which massively slows them down, and instead of being swept through the vessels at speed, they slowly roll along the lining of the vessel. This drastic slowing allows the neutrophil

to detect further cytokine signalling from macrophages, which tells it where the inflammatory battle is taking place. Chemicals called chemoattractants pull the neutrophil from inside the vessel through the vessel wall and into the tissues, towards the affected area. As the neutrophil leaves the circulation, it is activated, so it arrives ready for action. Much like macrophages, neutrophils are filled with lysosomes full of incredibly highly toxic compounds that rapidly and aggressively destroy pathogens they engulf. They also engulf pathogens in a far faster and more aggressive manner than macrophages do. Once a neutrophil has delivered as much of its phagocytic function as it can, it dies. When you have an infected wound that fills with pus, the pus is predominantly composed of dead neutrophils!

NATURAL KILLER CELLS

These are the final class of cells within innate immunity. They are not phagocytic, so they don't engulf pathogens. The natural killer (NK) cells are probably the most versatile cell line within the innate immune system. These potent cells can kill tumour cells, cells that have been infected with viruses, bacteria, parasites and fungi. They kill them by inducing them to commit suicide, rather than engulfing and digesting them as phagocytic cells do. NK cells do this by two major means. The first method is like a type of lethal injection. They penetrate the surface of the target (tumour cell or infected cell) using a substance called perforin. Once in, they deliver a burst of enzymes, such as granzyme B, that stimulate the target to commit suicide.

On other occasions, a protein on the outer surface of natural killer cells called fas ligand binds to a protein called fas on the outer surface of target cells. This binding induces the production of self-destruct enzymes in the target cell. NK cells identify their targets by markers displayed on the target cell – a bit like a 'kill' or 'don't kill' signal. Compounds such as MHC molecules on the outer surface of a cell, give a 'don't kill' signal to the NK cells. Other compounds such as specialised carbohydrate or protein molecules interact with the surface of NK cells to instigate a 'kill' response.

NK cells work in tandem with macrophages. During infection, for example, the initial cytokines released will bind to NK cells and tell them that a battle needs to be waged. The NK cells will respond by producing other cytokines, such as interferons, which activate macrophages. Activated macrophages, as you'll remember, can recruit neutrophils. Activated macrophages also secrete substances such as TNF, that stimulate NK cells to increase their expression of interferons, making the whole response more aggressive.

B CELLS

B cells are one of the major cell classes responsible for adaptive immunity. This is the branch of the immune system that develops and recognises pathogens and develops resistance to them. B cell production in the body is vast. We produce almost a billion of them a day! As the B cells develop, and before they make their way out into the body, they begin to manufacture several distinctive proteins that are bound within their membrane. These proteins function as antigen receptors, capable of recognising specific antigens. Antigens are substances that are recognised as foreign and that provoke immune responses. The way B cells are activated and play their role is truly fascinating. The B cell receptors described earlier bind to antigens. These antigens may be circulating, but most often are delivered by antigen-presenting cells such as macrophages. Some of the antigen is then taken into the B cell, where it is broken into fragments and then combined with MHC. The antigen fragment/MHC combination is then displayed on the outside of the B cell. At this point, another group of cells – T helper cells – recognises the antigen/MHC combination, and starts to communicate with the B cell displaying it. This communication then allows the B cells to proliferate and differentiate (morph and change). B cells can differentiate into a cell called a plasma cell. Plasma cells secrete antibodies to the antigen. These cells differentiate at an astounding rate and a few days after exposure to an antigen, there is a clone army of plasma cells secreting hundreds of millions of antibodies.

T CELLS

The T cells are the other major players in the adaptive immune system. Like B cells, as they mature they develop specialised receptors on their outer surface. These receptors are slightly different from the B cell ones. They are designed to recognise the antigen/ MHC complexes displayed on the outer surface of B cells (described above). There are millions of different types of T cells, all with receptors that recognise different antigen/MHC complexes. T cells require two stages to become activated. Binding to an antigen/MHC complex is the first stage. The second stage is referred to as co-stimulation. This co-stimulation usually comes from cytokines released by other cells. When these two stages have both been reached, the T cell can then proliferate (divide many times) and differentiate (develop into highly specialised cells).

There are three main types of T cells. T helper cells pretty much live up to their name. They assist the immune response in many ways, mostly due to their cytokine production. Within a few hours of activation, T helper cells begin to secrete cytokines,

an important one being interleukin-2 (IL-2). This cytokine is needed for virtually every conceivable immunological reaction. It is an important co-stimulator, and enhances the activation of T cells, B cells and natural killer cells.

Cytotoxic T cells are a far more aggressive variety. They can destroy problematic cells. These could be body cells affected by viruses or some tumour cells. T cells also attack transplanted organs (which is why transplant patients need immunosuppressant drugs). To get into this cytolytic (cell destroying) state cytotoxic T cells rely on co-stimulation by IL-2 (secreted by T helper cells).

ANTIBODIES

These wonderful compounds deserve their own paragraph. Even though they are not cells, but by-products of cells, they are a fundamental part of adaptive immunity. Also known as immunoglobulins, antibodies recognise antigens on the surface of foreign or problematic agents that trigger an immune response. When antibodies recognise the antigen, they bind to it. This creates a tag, a bit like sticking a giant flag in it, that signals to the relevant part of the immune system to attack the problematic invader or cell.

THE GUT FLORA – THE MISSING LINK IN IMMUNITY

The gut flora or micro biome is truly a wonderful thing. There are more bacterial cells in our bodies than human cells. We harbour an estimated 100 trillion bacterial cells. That's a number that is almost impossible to comprehend. These bacteria aren't there to cause a problem. Far from it. We have a symbiotic relationship with them, meaning that the relationship is mutually beneficial. In the digestive chapter I explained the incredible role that bacteria in the gut play in regulating multiple aspects of digestive health, from regulating peristalsis, through to housekeeping and nutrient synthesis. However, an area of research into gut flora that has really started to accelerate in recent years is the role that it plays in systemic immunity. It truly is the missing link in immunity.

The link between gut flora and immunity was initially observed when mice raised in completely sterile, germ-free environments (i.e. not exposed to any bacteria at all so their own bacterial colony was non-existent) displayed significant immunological deficiencies. Most noticeable were very poorly developed lymphoid tissues and lower numbers of immunological cells in key areas of their bodies. This led to the further discovery that the health of the gut flora was directly associated with the health of the immune system, and that specific bacterial strains activated specific immune cell lines

such as regulatory T cells. But how can a bacterial colony that lives in the gut affect an immune cell in the big toe? The truth is, at this stage, we simply don't know, but it seems almost certain that it involves an interaction between gut flora and gut associated lymphoid tissue (GALT).

GALT is made up of several different types of tissue throughout the entire digestive tract. Of most interest is a group of tissue patches called Peyer's patches. These are clusters of lymphoid nodules that can be seen as surveillance stations. Our digestive tract is an obvious route into the body for opportunistic pathogens, so as a region it must be tightly monitored. Peyer's patches relay information from within the gut to the rest of the immune system via chemical messengers. It is most likely that this is the level at which gut flora communicate with the rest of the immune system. This interaction with Peyer's patches sets off a series of systemic chemical messages that can activate, stimulate, reduce or switch off. While the science is in its infancy and the details of modes of action are still being investigated, supporting gut flora will always be a major part of any programme to support and enhance immunity.

DIET AND THE IMMUNE SYSTEM

Nutrition can play a fundamental role in the health and functioning of the immune system. Sometimes this can be as simple as supplying adequate nutrients for normal cell function, right through to directly stimulating and regulating specific immunological functions.

POLYSACCHARIDES

Polysaccharides are very large, complex sugar molecules. They are a type of sugar that in many cases is not broken down and utilised in the same manner as other sugars (at least the variety that we are concerned with here). They play a host of other biological roles, from acting as prebiotic agents, through to delivering immunomodulatory activity. Polysaccharides may prove to be the most exciting dietary component for immunomodulation, particularly the beta glucans found in mushrooms. Beta glucans have been studied for over 40 years. Much of this research has been done in Japan and the USA. These compounds have been shown to have a staggering effect upon immune function.

Polysaccharides are known to stimulate the production of NK cells, and also regu-

late T helper (Th) cells in some interesting ways. For many years it was believed that beta glucans delivered their activity on a kind of lock and key basis: receptor sites on the surface of specific leukocytes bound with beta glucan to affect the cells, which had an impact on their behaviour. However, this theory was scuppered when beta glucan was found intact in stool samples. It came through the digestive tract intact, yet still delivered its physiological effects of increasing NK cell numbers and interacting with Th. How did it do this? By interacting with the Peyer's patches! Remember, the Peyer's patch is like a surveillance station which monitors gut contents, and continually reports on them to the immune system. When the polysaccharides pass over the Peyer's patches, they seem to trigger some kind of chain reaction, almost like an alarm response. Exactly why this occurs is yet to be determined, but one of the theories is that mushroom polysaccharides are similar in structure to polysaccharides displayed on the outer surface of some types of bacteria. Immune cell lines residing in the Peyer's patches detect this as a bacterial attack, and begin to send out chemical messengers called cytokines to recruit and stimulate the correct immunological responses. This sequence of events is believed to be the key.

The best sources of beta glucan polysaccharides are shiitake, oyster and maitake mushrooms.

THE ROLE OF ZINC

Zinc is a very common ingredient in many cold and flu formulae – and for good reason. Some nutrients that are known to interact with immune function seem to have performed haphazardly in clinical trials for treating the common cold. However, zinc has consistently performed very well in trials, delivering a reduction in the duration and severity of colds and upper respiratory tract infections. So how does it deliver these effects? Zinc is used by most of the white blood cells within our immune system to code their genes. These genes regulate all the internal processes that control the way in which the white blood cells respond to pathogens and troubled tissues. Zinc is also used to regulate phagocytosis and the production of cytokines. Zinc also has an antimicrobial effect and is found in the mucous secretions of the upper respiratory tract.

The best sources of zinc are shellfish, pumpkin seeds, eggs, beef, almonds, cashews and cheese.

VITAMIN C

Vitamin C is probably the best-known nutrient when it comes to immune health. Unlike zinc, vitamin C often performs poorly in trials focused on treating the common cold. That being said, vitamin C is still an important nutrient for the overall health and functioning of the immune system, regardless of whether it shortens the duration of a cold or not. It affects immune function in several ways. First, vitamin C stimulates the production and activity of neutrophils, phagocytes and leukocytes. It stimulates their motility as well as the phagocytic processes. Several cell lines also accumulate vitamin C to protect them from oxidative damage during their normal responses when faced with pathogens. Vitamin C also regulates a specific immunological response called the oxidative burst. During this response leukocytes release a cloud of reactive oxygen species when faced with pathogens.

The best sources of vitamin C are peppers, spinach, broccoli, goji berries, kiwi fruit and citrus fruit.

ESSENTIAL FATTY ACIDS (EFAS)

The essential fatty acids omega 3 and omega 6 are very closely linked to immune function for several distinct reasons. First, as mentioned in the heart module, they play a key role in the regulation of the inflammatory response. Inflammation serves several purposes in immunity, such as increasing the passage of white blood cells into tissues. This is done by dilating the blood vessels, making them more porous and allowing white blood cells to squeeze through and enter infected tissues. Inflammation also draws our attention to an affected area. Fatty acids influence inflammation drastically. Different fatty acids influence inflammation in different ways, due to their metabolic end products – a class of compounds called prostaglandins. There are three types of prostaglandins: series 1, series 2 and series 3. Series 1 and 3 prostaglandins reduce inflammation, whereas series 2 prostaglandins activate and exacerbate inflammation. Different fatty acids are metabolised to form different types of prostaglandins. Omega 6 fatty acids are metabolised to form the pro-inflammatory series 2 prostaglandins. Omega 3 fatty acids, particularly EPA, are metabolised to form series 3 prostaglandins.

There is another group of newly discovered inflammatory mediators called resolvins, made from omega 3 fatty acids: E-series resolvins from EPA, and D-series resolvins from DHA. These compounds reduce active inflammation. When there is excessive inflammation, increasing intake of omega 3 fatty acids will have a notable anti-inflammatory effect, due to the increased expression of series 1 and 3 prostaglandins and the resolvins. Essential fatty acids also benefit immune function because of their importance to cell membranes. EFAs are incorporated into cell membranes and modulate vital cellular processes such as cell signalling and receptor function.

The best sources of essential fatty acids are oily fish, nuts and seeds.

OTHER IMPORTANT NUTRIENTS

Other nutrients are also important for healthy immunity, but don't warrant their own paragraph. Vitamin E, for example, regulates B and T lymphocyte function. Vitamins A, B1, B6, B12 and folic acid are all vital for healthy white cell function.

KEY FOODS FOR IMMUNE HEALTH

GARLIC

Garlic contains several elements beneficial to the immune system. Many are simple nutrients such as the B vitamins and vitamin C. However, there are other compounds that are non-nutritional but biologically active that give garlic its age-old reputation as an antiviral. These are sulphur-based compounds that are responsible for the pungent smell of garlic. These substances, once through the digestive system, can only be removed from the body via one route and one route alone. They aren't water soluble so don't get excreted via the urine. They aren't fat soluble so they don't leave via the bowel. They are removed via the respiratory tract. That is why a night out at a restaurant can leave you smelling like Buffy the Vampire Slayer's pocket. As these substances are breathed out, they can pick off susceptible bugs and viruses that cling to the mucous membranes.

GOJI BERRIES

Some utterly ridiculous claims have been made about these berries, but they are rich in polysaccharides similar to those found in shiitake mushrooms. While they do not have the same evidence base as shiitake mushrooms do, there is suggestion that their polysaccharides may also be immunomodulatory.

SHIITAKE MUSHROOMS

These are the richest available sources of potent polysaccharides available in the UK. They are potent sugars that can interact with lymphoid tissue in the gut and set off a systemic immune response, such as elevating NK cell numbers.

PUMPKIN SEEDS

These are a great source of the vital mineral zinc, which is used by our white blood cells to code genes that then help to regulate the responses to pathogens instigated by such cells.

SHELLFISH

Prawns and scallops especially are also very rich sources of zinc.

RECIPES FOR A HEALTHY IMMUNE SYSTEM
– TOP INGREDIENTS –

The recipes that follow contain ingredients which have medicinal benefits for the immune system. Here is a rundown of these 'star' ingredients and their medicinal properties:

CHILLI (pages 117, 119, 120) is a great ingredient if you have a cold. That's because it is a decongestant. Have you ever eaten something spicy and found that your nose starts running? There it is in action.

GARLIC (pages 116, 117, 119, 120, 123) contains potent antiviral volatile oils. These give garlic its notorious odour that lingers on the breath. As we breathe out these oils, they can destroy susceptible pathogens that can linger on the mucous membranes within the respiratory tract.

GINGER (page 117) delivers an anti-inflammatory effect by interrupting the conversion of arachidonic acid into the series 2 prostaglandins that trigger and worsen inflammation. The bunged-up feeling we often have during a cold is usually caused by inflammation of the mucous membranes.

GOJI BERRIES (pages 115, 116, 117) have been highlighted by the media in recent years, and some astounding and notably far-fetched claims have been made about them. They have been viewed as the ultimate superfood. While much of this can be considered hype, goji berries do have some interesting effects upon the immune system. Like many medicinal plants and mushrooms, they contain a group of special sugars called polysaccharides. They are known to powerfully stimulate the immune system. They do this by causing an increase in the production of white blood cells. The second fact about goji berries – and the one

I find most interesting – is their high levels of the trace element germanium. Germanium is one of the hardest trace elements to find in our modern diet and is of vital importance when it comes to the health of the immune system. Germanium is an important nutrient in the regulation of a group of cells called CD4 cells. These cells can be viewed as the conductor of an orchestra. They tell all the other cells of the immune system what to do, when and how, and play a pivotal role in the organisation of almost every immune response. CD4 cells are affected by HIV infection, and a decline in these cells is what causes the immune system's demise in this awful disease.

MUSSELS (page 119) are packed with zinc. This important mineral is involved in hundreds of chemical reactions daily. It is used by our white blood cells to code genes that are used to regulate the way in which they respond to pathogens and damaged or infected tissues.

PUMPKIN SEEDS (page 115) are one of my favourite nibbles to have around the house. They are very high in another important trace mineral: zinc! Zinc has been widely researched in recent years, especially in the context of immunity. One of the key roles this wonderful mineral plays is the regulation of the functioning of individual white blood cells. It does this by ensuring correct functioning of their individual DNA – the internal code that programmes every func-

tion of every cell in every tissue. A healthy, fully functioning DNA means a healthy, fully functioning white blood cell, able to deliver its best performance when faced with an invader. Pumpkin seeds are also a very rich source of the chemical cucurbitin, which is a powerful antiviral and anti-parasitic agent. This makes them very useful if you have a case of food poisoning, when an infective agent has found its way into the body via the digestive tract. Pumpkin seeds have a long history as a traditional remedy for such infections.

PRAWNS and **SCALLOPS** (pages 120, 123) are packed with the mineral zinc, used by white blood cells to regulate responses to pathogens. Zinc is one nutrient that has consistently performed well in clinical trials tackling the common cold. Although vitamin C has delivered mixed results in terms of its ability to reduce the duration and severity of the common cold, zinc has shown consistent benefit.

SHIITAKE MUSHROOMS (pages 117, 120) contain a type of sugar called a polysaccharide, that has been widely studied in Asia and the US for over 40 years. These polysaccharides have been shown to increase the production of certain white blood cells in the immune system called natural killer cells. They have also been shown to increase the motility of white cells to the site of infection.

GOJI BERRY AND PUMPKIN SEED ENERGY BOMBS

MAKES 8

1 heaped tablespoon
   coconut oil
3 handfuls pumpkin seeds
3 handfuls goji berries

MEDICINAL PROPERTIES

GOJI BERRIES
PUMPKIN SEEDS

These provide a simple and easy snack, high in nutrients and energy, that can be eaten at any time of the day. They are especially useful if you are suffering from the sniffles, as they are packed with immune-boosting chemicals and nutrients. The method for making these tasty treats will probably remind you of making cornflake cakes as a child.

1. Quarter fill a saucepan with water and place a heat-proof glass bowl on top to create a bain-marie. Put the coconut oil in the bowl and heat gently.

2. Meanwhile, put the pumpkin seeds and goji berries into a food processor, and process at a medium speed until they have a coarse texture.

3. Once the coconut oil is melted, add it to the goji berries and pumpkin seeds, and mix thoroughly to give a sticky but firm mixture.

4. Roll into bite-sized balls, place on a plate and refrigerate until firm.

GOJI BERRY HUMMUS

SERVES 2

400g can chickpeas, drained
1 large clove garlic, roughly
  chopped
3 tablespoons goji berries,
  soaked
juice of half a lemon
3 tablespoons olive oil
sea salt

This simple dip is an interesting twist on a classic: fruity and rich. You can also try adding different spices to it like cumin or coriander.

Put the chickpeas, garlic, goji berries and two tablespoons of the soaking water into a food processor, with the lemon juice and olive oil, plus a good pinch of salt. Blend into a smooth dip.

MEDICINAL PROPERTIES

GARLIC
GOJI BERRIES

TURBO-CHARGED CHICKEN SOUP

SERVES 2–3

1 large red onion, finely
chopped
4 cloves garlic, finely chopped
1 red chilli, finely chopped
2.5cm piece ginger, peeled
and finely chopped
1 carrot, finely chopped
olive oil, for frying
5 or 6 dried shiitake
mushrooms
3 tablespoons goji berries
3 chicken legs
300ml vegetable stock
sea salt

The old classic given a boot!

1. Sauté the onion, garlic, chilli, ginger and carrot in a
little olive oil with a good pinch of salt, until the onion
has softened.

2. Add the shiitake mushrooms and goji berries.

3. Using a cleaver or heavy knife, cut into the meat
and bone of the chicken legs to expose the inside of
the bone. Add to the other ingredients with the stock,
simmer for about 40 minutes, then allow to cool.

4. Once cooled, remove the chicken legs and strip the
meat off the bones. Discard the bones and replace
the meat in the soup. Warm through before serving.

MEDICINAL PROPERTIES

CHILLI
GARLIC
GINGER
GOJI BERRIES

MUSSELS IN TOMATO CHILLI SAUCE

**SERVES 2 AS A MAIN,
4 AS A STARTER**

1 red onion, halved and finely
  chopped
2 cloves garlic, finely chopped
1 small red chilli, chopped
olive oil, for frying
400g tin chopped tomatoes
1kg mussels, beards removed
  (discard open mussels that
  don't close when tapped)
sea salt

Simple and flavoursome – the key to all good food,
I think. This recipe is no exception.

1. Sauté the onion, garlic and chilli in a little olive oil,
along with a good pinch of salt, until the onion softens.

2. Add the tomatoes and simmer for 10–15 minutes,
until the sauce thickens and reduces and the flavour
intensifies.

3. Add the mussels, cover with a lid and simmer for
2–3 minutes. Stir the mussels well to ensure that they
are well covered with sauce. Simmer for another 2–3
minutes until all the mussels have opened.

MEDICINAL PROPERTIES
CHILLI
GARLIC
MUSSELS

PRAWN, SHIITAKE AND SPRING ONION SPEEDY NOODLES

SERVES 2

2 bundles soba noodles
3 cloves garlic, finely chopped
½ red onion, finely sliced
½ red chilli, finely chopped
3 spring onions, sliced
  longways
olive oil, for frying
220g cooked king prawns
10 shiitake mushrooms, sliced
1 teaspoon honey
1 tablespoon soy sauce
2 teaspoons sesame oil
½ teaspoon Chinese five
  spice powder

This is a quick, simple dinner recipe that tastes wonderful – better than a takeaway I'd say! Soba noodles come already measured into single portion bundles, which makes life easier.

1. Put the soba noodles in a saucepan and cover with boiling water. Simmer until the noodles are soft.

2. In a large frying pan or a wok stir-fry the garlic, red onion, chilli and spring onions in a little olive oil, until the onion has softened.

3. Add the prawns and shiitake mushrooms and continue to stir-fry until the mushrooms are soft.

4. Drain the noodles, add them to the pan and toss to ensure everything is evenly mixed. Add the honey, soy sauce, sesame oil and five spice powder and toss well again.

MEDICINAL PROPERTIES

CHILLI
GARLIC
PRAWNS
SHIITAKE MUSHROOMS

SEAFOOD LINGUINE

SERVES 2

125g linguine
10g butter
1 clove garlic, very finely
    chopped
1 tablespoon white wine
2 teaspoons grated Parmesan
125g uncooked prawns
125g uncooked scallops
    (without roe)
sea salt
green salad, to serve

MEDICINAL PROPERTIES

GARLIC
PRAWNS AND SCALLOPS

This is such a simple dish, but it is utter heaven.

1. Put the pasta in a saucepan, cover with boiling water and simmer until cooked.

2. Melt the butter in a frying pan over a low heat and sauté the garlic gently for a minute or two. Add the wine and Parmesan, along with a good pinch of salt.

3. Add the prawns and scallops and sauté for 4–5 minutes, stirring frequently. Add a tablespoon of the pasta water and mix well.

4. Drain the pasta and add it to the seafood mix. Toss well to ensure that the pasta is completely covered, and the seafood is mixed through it.

5. Serve with a green salad.

GENERAL TIPS TO REMEMBER FOR A HEALTHY IMMUNE SYSTEM

AVOID REFINED SUGAR. Simple, refined sugars, such as the white sugar you may put in your tea, or find in white bread and white pasta, are terrible for our health on so many levels. Sugar and refined carbohydrates are renowned for greatly reducing our immunity. Studies have shown that even an intake of about 35 grams of sugar (the amount in a can of fizzy drink) is enough to cause a fifty per cent reduction in the ability of phago-cytes (a specific type of white blood cell) to engulf and destroy bacteria. Sugar is also known to slow down the rate at which white blood cells migrate to the site of infection, and is also believed to slow down the pro-duction of white blood cells in the thymus gland. If you need to use sweeteners, go for raw agave nectar, yacon syrup or a good quality honey. Swap white bread, rice and pasta for wholegrain varieties.

EAT THE RAINBOW. Brightly coloured fruits and vegetables are often the magic bullets for all-round health. Each vivid colour represents different spectrums of phyto-chemicals and antioxidants. Many of these brightly coloured compounds help to protect tissues from damage, reduce inflammation and give the immune system a helping hand by enhancing the overall health of the tissues in general.

STAY HYDRATED. Staying properly hydrated is important for many reasons. In the context of immunity, being properly hydrated will help in the removal of waste products from the body. This will reduce the burden on tissues, so will help to leave them healthier and less open to infection.

THE JOINTS

Diseases of the joints and skeleton are on the increase. While the highest percentage of these are suffered by older generations, some diseases – such as rickets which was, at one point, almost completely eradicated – have started to rear their ugly heads again among the young. Here in the UK, more than three million people live with osteoporosis. Cases of rickets have risen from 0.34 per 100,000 children between 1991 and 1996, to 3.16 cases per 100,000 between 2007 and 2011, which may not sound a lot, but is the highest it has been in 50 years. In the UK there are 400,000 adults with rheumatoid arthritis. While this certainly isn't a pattern of disease ultimately caused by nutritional factors, diet and nutrition are, of course, key areas in their management.

STRUCTURE OF BONES

Developing a clear understanding of the structure and function of a system will explain the role nutrition can play in both the cause of a disease and its management. The place to start is the basic structure of the bone, before looking at how the physiological system works.

THE DIAPHYSIS

The diaphysis is essentially the shaft or the main body of the bone. It is composed of very compact bone that surrounds bone marrow.

THE EPIPHYSIS

The epiphysis are the two ends of long bones. These areas are filled with spongy bone – a criss-cross lattice structure.

THE MEDULLARY CAVITY

This is the central cavity that runs through the diaphysis, with its walls of compact bone. It is the area that holds the bone marrow.

ENDOSTEUM

The endosteum is a thin membrane that lines the inside of the medullary cavity, and is host to the highest number of osteoclasts (see below).

ARTICULAR CARTILAGE

The articular cartilage is a layer of cartilage that covers the epiphysis, where the bone becomes part of a joint. The cartilage is there to prevent potential friction against two bony surfaces, and to offer lubrication so that the joint moves freely and easily.

PERIOSTIUM

The periostium is a tough sheath of connective tissue that covers the surface of the bone. This protective sheath contains bone-forming cells that enable the bone to grow in diameter and thickness. It also helps with the transport of nutrients into the bone, and is an attachment point for ligaments and tendons.

CELL TYPES IN BONE TISSUE

OSTEOBLASTS

Osteoblasts are bone-building cells that are highly active during growth spurts in the bones. These cells secrete the structural protein collagen and other substances that lay down the matrix of bone tissue. This matrix is a criss-cross lattice of structural fibres which eventually becomes hardened with minerals. As osteoblasts secrete collagen and build the matrix, they become trapped within their own secretions and so are trapped within the matrix. At this point, they become osteocytes.

OSTEOCYTES

Osteocytes are mature bone cells, and the main types of cells within bones. They are responsible for the ongoing metabolic functions of bone, such as the exchange of nutrients and waste with the blood.

OSTEOCLASTS

Osteoclasts are freakishly large cells. They are made from as many as 50 monocytes (as explained in the immunity chapter) all fused together. These giant cells are found mostly in the endosteum – the inner membrane that lines the inner surface of the medullary cavity. The side of the cells that face the bone have a surface that resembles a frilly, ruffled border. This creates greater surface area. The ruffled border is where the cells release lysozomal enzymes and acids that break down the collagen network and mineral deposits of the bone. This breaking down of the bone is referred to as resorption and is a normal part of the growth and development, and repair of the bone.

DISEASES OF THE BONES

Diseases of the bones are serious! Though mostly associated with the elderly, disorders of the bones can affect all age groups in numerous ways. Some diseases which were once drastically reduced are starting to rear their ugly head again, and this is the result of external factors. More on that later. Let's start with osteoporosis. This thinning of bone affects more than three million people in the UK alone. Nutritional deficiency diseases such as osteomalacia and rickets are also on the increase, which should not be happening in this day and age. There are many diseases of the bones, a lot of which have genetic links or complex pathologies. Those discussed below are the ones in which nutrition can have an impact, so be aware that this isn't an exhaustive list of bone diseases, but covers those our diet can affect.

OSTEOPOROSIS

Osteoporosis is probably the best-known and most widely discussed of the bone diseases and is very serious indeed. It is essentially a thinning of the bone. During childhood our bones break down and rebuild very rapidly as part of their normal growth cycle. This normal cycle of events slows down as we get older. Bones stop growing in length between the ages of 16 and 18 and they stop growing in thickness and developing their density around the late 20s. When we hit about 35, our bone density begins to reduce gradually. This is normal. Osteoporosis, however, represents a notable imbalance in the rate of bone resorption to bone remineralisation. Osteoporosis develops due to three main mechanisms, and often there is an interplay between the three. These three factors are inadequate peak bone mass (i.e. the peak density that bone reaches in the early 20s, which can be heavily influenced by early nutrition and lifestyle), excessive bone resorption, and inadequate formation of new bone during remodelling.

One of the key times when osteoporosis can become a huge problem for women is during and after the menopause. During this time, oestrogen levels plummet. This drop in oestrogen stimulates osteoclastogenesis – an increase in production of osteoclasts – which in turn causes an increase in bone resorption. The drop in oestrogen also stimulates the production of certain cytokines (chemical messengers) such as interleukin-6 in the marrow which also stimulates bone turnover. This increased breakdown of bone causes blood levels of calcium to rise as the mineral is liberated from the skeletal matrix during resorption. The body responds to this by reducing the activity of the parathyroid hormone (PTH). This is the most important regulator of calcium in the body. Reducing PTH increases the removal of calcium via the urine, a status known as calciuria. Reduced PTH also suppresses the production of calcitriol – the hormonally active metabolite of vitamin D. One of the main roles calcitriol plays is regulating blood concentrations of calcium. It does this by reducing urinary calcium loss and promoting the intestinal absorption of calcium. This creates a state in which available calcium becomes sparse, which when coupled with accelerated bone resorption, creates a serious problem.

Bone density loss and osteoporosis aren't purely a menopausal issue, although menopause does result in a much more rapid and aggressive onset. It is something that can develop with age. As we age there is a gradual decline in kidney and intestinal function. This affects the rate at which calcium is excreted via the urine, and also the amount of calcium that we are able to absorb via the gut. Also, our diets tend to become a little more restricted with age, and nutrient levels drop with reduced appetite, leading to less dietary calcium being available. The final blow is that vitamin D production in the skin decreases, and many older people find that they spend less time outdoors. If you bring all these factors together, you end up with decreased serum calcium. Now, we met PTH earlier. This hormone directly responds to serum calcium levels (calcium is vital in muscle function and all cellular signalling, not just bone). If the level becomes too high it facilitates calcium removal, if levels become too low, it does all it can to get the calcium back up as described above. However, with reduced calcitriol expression as a result of lack of vitamin D, and reduced intake and absorption of calcium, there is only one store for the body to draw on – the biggest calcium storage depot of them all, the skeleton. In this set of circumstances, PTH levels begin to rise, which leads to an accelerated bone remodelling to liberate calcium and restore serum concentrations. With age, osteoblast activity also reduces notably. So we have a situation where there is accelerated bone resorption, coupled with reduced remineralisation and reduced levels of the structural materials needed to rebuild the bone. Other diseases also bring about an increased risk of osteoporosis, such as hyperparathyroidism, renal diseases, anorexia and malabsorption diseases, but in terms of nutritional management, the big two – menopause and advancing age – are the ones that are most likely to be influenced by changes in diet and lifestyle.

OSTEOMALACIA AND RICKETS

Osteomalacia and rickets are basically the same condition, and are a consequence of poor bone mineralisation. Both conditions result in a softening of the bones due to insufficient levels of phosphate and calcium deposited within them. In adults the condition is called osteomalacia and in children, the more severe and slightly different version is called rickets. In the case of osteomalacia, the poor bone mineralisation can be a result of several factors similar to those outlined previously for osteoporosis. There can be an elevation in parathyroid hormone, for example due to hyperparathyroidism, reduced calcium intake or poor calcium utilisation and decreased vitamin D levels. It very often starts with aches and pains in the lower part of the spine and the thighs, before eventually spreading to the arms. This often leads to difficulties in walking properly,

resulting in a waddling gait. Bones can bend and flattening of the pelvis can occur.

Rickets is in essence the same issue – poor bone mineralisation, but it occurs before epiphyseal closure, the stopping of bone growth. Reduced mineralisation at this growth stage can have much more severe and noticeable consequences. The weight bearing down upon the softened bones can lead to deformities. In toddlers this can often be seen as bowed legs and in older children as knock knees. It can also result in cranial, spinal and pelvic deformities, as well as growth disturbances.

In some parts of the world rickets is very common. This is because it is most often associated with severe malnutrition. It is, after all, a vitamin D deficiency issue. However, in recent years, the UK has seen a vast increase in the number of cases of rickets in children from all backgrounds. How so? Well, much of this has come from the overuse of sunblock. Don't worry, I am not for a minute suggesting throwing sunscreen away, but perhaps the extent to which sunblock is used should be reconsidered. We need *some* sunlight exposure. That's for sure. Just a small amount, ten minutes in the sun when it's not too hot, can help us to synthesise vitamin D. The other reason rickets is beginning to rear its ugly head again is that the few food sources of vitamin D are seldom eaten by a big proportion of the public. Full fat milk, butter and oily fish such as sardines, herrings and salmon are all rich sources, and aside from salmon, they are not very widely consumed.

NUTRITIONAL MANAGEMENT OF BONE DISEASES

Nutrition can play a fundamental role in these diseases. Part of the therapeutic picture is prevention, and part intervention. Preventing and treating the diseases of the bone described above requires a blanket approach. In terms of prevention, it is wise to start taking in adequate levels of the key nutrients from the late 20s to the early 30s. In terms of management, as soon as a diagnosis is made, efforts to improve the status of these nutrients must begin immediately.

CALCIUM

This is the obvious place to start – the basic structural component of the skeleton. It is the primary mineral laid down within the skeletal matrix to harden the skeleton so it can offer support and withstand force, but also to create a store of this ubiquitous mineral. While it is the most abundant structural material in the skeleton, it may in fact be the least important nutritional component when it comes to skeletal health. Compare calcium to the bricks on a building site. While it is the key structural component, without a team of builders and bricklayers, nothing will happen – it will just sit there. Well, calcium without all the other auxiliary nutrients needed to do something with it is as good as useless. As I have explained previously, most of the pathological processes

of osteoporosis and osteomalacia/rickets involve the reduced availability of calcium at some stage, whether through lack of dietary intake, lack of absorption or lack of mobilisation to where it is needed. A great deal of this is regulated by other auxiliary nutrients. A good intake of calcium is essential, especially during key times such as infancy and senior years, but don't see calcium as the be-all and end-all.

VITAMIN D

Vitamin D is one of the big nutritional darlings of recent times, and a nutrient that has been the focus of a great deal of research. It isn't strictly a vitamin; it is more of a hormone as it is synthesised in the body, and then delivers its actions in sites away from its point of synthesis. The primary source of vitamin D for humans is the conversion of cholesterol into vitamin D when exposing the skin to ultraviolet radiation – i.e. sunshine! Now, here in the UK we are in a sticky spot from the start as the sun is very often a rumour for most of the year. When vitamin D enters the body via our food, or is synthesised in the skin, it is metabolically inactive. It goes through several stages of enzymatic conversion in the liver, where it is converted into calcidiol, and then in the kidneys where it is converted into calcitriol, before it can be used. Calcitriol really has one primary objective, and that is to increase the concentration of calcium in the blood. If blood calcium goes down, then calcitriol responds by increasing absorption of dietary calcium and also reducing calcium loss via the kidneys. This in itself can encourage greater bone remineralisation as more calcium becomes available.

MAGNESIUM

Magnesium is possibly one of the most overlooked minerals in the whole bone-health picture. Magnesium deficiency is one of the most common nutrition deficiencies in the Western world. One of the reasons for this is that it is most abundant in green leafy vegetables, and let's face it, how many people chow down on huge amounts of greens every day? Couple this with the fact that it is used in more than 1,000 enzymatic reactions in the body, meaning that stores can be used up easily, and you set the stage for deficiency. Sixty per cent of the body's magnesium stores are found within the skeleton. In terms of its role in bone health, it is linked to facilitating enzymatic reactions. One of the first areas this comes into play is in the conversion of vitamin D into its active form. There is an enzyme that is required for forming calcium crystals within the skeleton called alkaline phosphatase. Magnesium is an important component for activating this enzyme, and even a mild deficiency can lead to abnormal crystal formation.

ZINC

The mineral zinc is seldom discussed in the context of bone health, but in recent years it has come to light that it is an important factor in the overall health of the skeleton. Zinc is an important cofactor in the stimulation of osteoblasts, and can even stimulate the production of new osteoblasts. Zinc seems to aid in the suppression of excessive osteoclast activity and can help trigger apoptosis (programmed cell death) in old osteoclasts. Like magnesium, zinc is also involved in the activity of the enzyme alkaline phosphatase.

THE ROLE OF THE JOINTS

The skeleton offers us strong stable support, keeps us upright and holds our shape, and protects our vital organs from damage. However, our bones are not flexible enough to bend and move around when we make the thousands of individual movements we do every day. For this we need a system that allows movement, be it the full range of motion, or just the slightest bit of added flexibility. Enter the joints! Our joints allow movement between two bony surfaces without a bone fracturing, or two bony surfaces rubbing together. There are several different types of joints and gaining a basic understanding of these can help you to contextualise the way in which nutrition can be utilised as a therapeutic intervention.

Our joints are classified in two distinct

ways: by their structure and by their function. The structural classification varies according to whether there is a space between the two moving bones or not (a synovial cavity), and also the type of connective tissue binding the bones together. The functional classification varies according to the degree of movement a joint provides.

STRUCTURAL CLASSIFICATION

Fibrous joints: the bones are held together by a fibrous, collagen-rich fibres, and have no synovial cavity.

Cartilaginous joints: these bones are held together by cartilage, and again have no synovial cavity.

Synovial joints: the bones forming these joints have a synovial cavity. This is a fluid-filled capsule of connective tissue that allows cushioning and greater range of movement.

FUNCTIONAL CLASSIFICATION

Syntharthrosis: essentially an immovable joint.

Amphiarthosis: a slightly movable joint.

Diarthrosis: a type of joint that has an almost completely free range of movement.

Of all of these joints, the ones most susceptible to maladies other than trauma-based incident (e.g. a fracture) are the synovial joints. These undergo the most movement and are the most susceptible to wear and tear. They are also the ones that can be influenced by nutritional intervention.

SYNOVIAL JOINTS

These joints offer an almost complete range of movement. They have certain characteristics that set them apart from other joints. The main characteristic is the presence of a sealed space between the two bones that make the joint, known as the synovial cavity. The ends of the bones in a synovial joint are covered with articular cartilage to provide a lubricated surface and protection.

Within a synovial joint the articular capsule is a sleeve-like capsule that surrounds the whole joint, ensuring that the space between the bones remains sealed. The capsule also serves to keep the two bones connected to one another. The capsule is composed of two layers. The outer layer, the fibrous capsule, is made of very dense connective tissue. This tissue attaches to the periosteum of the bones of the joint. The fibrous capsule is both very flexible – to allow relatively unrestricted movement – yet incredibly strong, to offer sufficient support to prevent dislocation. The inner part of the articular capsule is known as the synovial membrane, and is made up of a softer connective tissue.

ARTICULAR CARTILAGE

A brief description of cartilage structure will help with understanding a little later on. It is composed of several elements. The first is its cells. These are called chondrocytes. These are surrounded by an extracellular matrix that holds them in place. This matrix is composed of water and key proteins such as collagen and glycosaminoglycans. The matrix is flexible and gives the articular cartilage the ability to compress and bear loads as the joint moves.

SYNOVIAL FLUID

The synovial membrane (inner part of the articular capsule) secretes a fluid called synovial fluid. This viscous pale fluid is said to resemble the white of an egg. It is made up of hyaluronic acid and interstitial fluid which offers lubrication and reduces friction within the joints. Synovial fluid also contains phagocytes that remove debris and metabolic waste that is a normal consequence of wear and tear within the joint.

DISEASES OF THE JOINTS

OSTEOARTHRITIS

Osteoarthritis is the name given to the type of joint degradation that involves normal wear and tear. It is the gradual decline of synovial joints, most typically weight-bearing joints. Primary osteoarthritis is a result of the natural ageing and decline of the cartilage. Osteoarthritis can also occur following injury or trauma to a joint at any age. In normal healthy cartilage, the extracellular matrix that holds chondrocytes in place is subject to an almost consistent breaking down and remodelling at a subtle level. Enzymes are secreted that degrade cartilage and other enzymes are released that synthesise fresh matrix, keeping the cartilage volume consistent. However, in osteoarthritis, the level of breakdown exceeds the level of synthesis. Protease enzymes such as collagenase break down the extracellular matrix. There is a loss of collagen, which brings a loss of flexibility that eventually leads to a breaking down of the cartilage. This begins as mild erosion and cracking within the superficial layer of the cartilage. It soon extends to the deeper layers, and eventually leads to large observable areas of cartilage destruction. This can leave areas of the articulating bones fully exposed so they begin to rub together, causing damage. When this occurs, the ends of the articular bone start to thicken to try and protect itself. This can lead to the growth of small, sometimes spiky projections called osteophytes which protrude and cause pain and decreased mobility within the joint. As the disease progresses, all other tissues within the joint can become more active. The synovium can thicken and start to secrete more synovial fluid, which can cause swelling and reduced movement in the joint. There can also be an increase in inflammatory mediators which may accelerate the chondrocytes' expression of protease enzymes and further worsen cartilage degradation. So, what nutritional strategies are there for osteoarthritis?

SUPPORT CARTILAGE: In an ideal world, being able to support cartilage significantly would be the greatest nutritional strategy of all for osteoarthritis. However, the evidence for how well this can be done is very poor indeed. One of the most popular supplements on the market, for example, is glucosamine. This is a combination of glucose and the amino acid glutamine. Glucosamine forms larger substances called glycosaminoglycans which form part of the extracellular matrix in cartilage. Some animal studies have suggested that glucosamine can stimulate the chondrocyte to decrease cartilage degradation, and also stimulate the synthesis of extracellular matrix. However, human studies have not shown the same results and currently there is little evidence that glucosamine is useful. I see no harm in using glucosamine supplements as there is no risk in doing so and they may well offer

benefit, but my main strategy is to ensure adequate vitamin C intake. This is one of the key nutrients involved in the production of collagen – one of the main structural load-bearing proteins within the extracellular matrix.

REDUCE INFLAMMATION: This is where nutrition really offers therapeutic value, giving great relief to sufferers with this painful condition. The key here is the manipulation of dietary fats, creating the right balancing act: raising omega 3 and reducing omega 6. Omega 3 and omega 6 fatty acids are both essential and we need them in our diet. Lack of either can cause serious problems. They are involved in everything from regulating cell membrane function, to hormonal health, to neurological function and immunological functions. Probably the most significant in terms of how they influence (either positively or negatively) the Western diet is their impact on inflammation. Essential fatty acids are metabolised through several enzymatic steps before they can become metabolically active. One of their key metabolic end products is a group of compounds called prostaglandins.

Prostaglandins are communication compounds that have a regulatory function in the body. One of the main things they regulate is the inflammatory response. There are three types of prostaglandin: series 1, series 2 and series 3. Series 1 and 3 reduce and switch off inflammation, with series 3 being the more aggressively anti-inflammatory.

Series 2, on the other hand, are powerfully pro-inflammatory and activate and exacerbate inflammation. Different fatty acids are metabolised to form different prostaglandins. Omega 3 fatty acids are metabolised to form series 1 and 3, with the fatty acid EPA elevating series 3 most notably, whereas omega 6 fatty acids are metabolised to form series 2 prostaglandins – the ones that activate and worsen inflammation.

So, the place to start is to reduce omega 6. This is easily done by using only two oils for cooking – olive oil and coconut oil. Most omega 6 fatty acids come from vegetable oils such as sunflower oil – the very oils that we were all encouraged to switch to for the good of our health. Olive and coconut oils contain no omega 6 fatty acids. The main fatty acid in olive oil is oleic acid (omega 9), and coconut oil has no unsaturated fatty acids in it at all. So using these two will help prevent excessive intake of omega 6.

The second part of the picture is to increase intake of omega 3 fatty acids. Omega 3 comes in several forms, one, called ALA, being the plant source. The best forms of omega 3 fatty acids which deliver benefit are EPA and DHA, found in abundance in oily fish such as salmon, trout, mackerel, herrings and so on. The plant source of omega 3 ALA has to be converted by several enzymatic processes into EPA and DHA. Human beings are notoriously poor at doing this. On average we convert about six per cent of dietary ALA into the more active long chain fatty acids EPA and DHA. Animals such as fish can do this conversion much more effectively than we can, and store these fats in their tissues preformed, making them ideal dietary sources of omega 3. However, don't write off ALA. Consuming it may offer anti-inflammatory benefit, even if we don't manage to convert it into any of the active EPA and DHA. How so? Well, this is because omega 3 and omega 6 both require the same pathways for their metabolism. Omega 6 goes through the same group of enzymes to be converted into series 2 prostaglandins as omega 3 does to become series 1 and 3. So, if you are reducing intake of 6, and then feeding in more ALA than omega 6, you won't necessarily be expressing much in the way of EPA and DHA, but you will block the conversion of omega 6 into series 2 prostaglandins so there will be fewer inflammatory mediators that exacerbate inflammation.

RHEUMATOID ARTHRITIS

Rheumatoid arthritis is a totally different disease. Rather than joint degradation as a result of what is considered normal wear and tear, rheumatoid arthritis can be seen as being an immune-mediated inflammatory disorder, in essence an 'autoimmune' issue in which the body's own immune system begins to attack the body's tissues! It isn't totally clear what triggers the immune system and creates this aggressive response to tissues in the joint, but once this occurs, cells of the immune system begin to produce antibodies to the synovium. This causes a cascade of inflammation within the joint that creates inflammatory damage within the articular cartilage. Once this inflammatory damage has become severe, a pannus begins to form. This is a thickening synovial tissue that grows over the inflamed articular cartilage. As immune-mediated immune responses continue to cause inflammation and chaos, the pannus continues to grow and cause erosions of the articular cartilage. The growing pannus can also lead to the destruction and invasion of the bone within the joint, which leads to joint deformity and a reduced range of motion of the joint.

Rheumatoid arthritis is quite an animal to tame. As there is a powerful autoimmune element, you will always be fighting that, and there is no strong evidence that the response itself can be regulated. That being said, it is possible to achieve an element of control over inflammation. The first move is to employ the methods described above: raising omega 3, reducing omega 6. There are also some interesting foods that can be added to the anti-inflammatory armoury. These are what we term the auxiliary foods.

GINGER: Ginger is one of the most powerful anti-inflammatories. The strong, spicy essential oils that give its spicy flavour have been shown by thousands of studies to interrupt certain aspects of the chemical reaction that occurs when inflammation is triggered. As mentioned earlier, the series 2 prostaglandins switch on and exacerbate inflammation. They are formed by converting arachidonic acid into the series 2 prostaglandins (excess omega 6 converts to arachidonic acid). The compounds in ginger inhibit the activity of the enzyme, called cyclo-oxygenase, that does this conversion. So, in essence it prevents the formation of pro-inflammatory compounds.

PINEAPPLE: Pineapple contains a very powerful enzyme called bromelain, which blocks certain aspects of the inflammatory response. Pineapple has a great track record for benefiting many painful inflammatory conditions. However, most of the bromelain is found in the tougher inner core of the pineapple, the bit that most of us throw away; in very ripe pineapples, though, it is sometimes edible.

TURMERIC: Turmeric is one of the kings of anti-inflammatory ingredients. The chemicals that give turmeric its vivid orange colour are a group of compounds called curcuminoids. These have been studied for decades and are known to reduce inflammation by blocking the enzyme involved in arachidonic acid conversion. Turmeric is very powerful indeed and some studies have compared the effectiveness of extracts of turmeric with some pharmaceutical drugs.

KEY FOODS FOR BONE HEALTH

YOGHURT

Yoghurt is one of the top calcium-rich foods. It is pretty well established that dairy products contain plenty of calcium, but some of them are not well tolerated. For example, many people have issues with the milk sugar lactose. In yoghurt, the lactose has been fermented and converted into lactic acid (which gives yoghurt its sharp flavour), so people with mild lactose issues are generally fine with yoghurt. The fact that it is cultured gives it an added boost as it helps digestive health by supporting the gut flora. A good plain natural yoghurt (not the sugar-laden ones that dominate the supermarket shelves) contains roughly 285mg of calcium per 150g serving!

FULL FAT CHEESES

For those who choose to eat it, having good quality full fat cheese in your diet is valuable. Forget low fat cheeses, full fat is the way to go, just don't eat too much. Why full fat? Well, within the fat lies a vitally important fat-soluble vitamin – vitamin D. Take away the fat and you take away the vitamin D. Then cheese also contains a reasonable quantity of calcium.

However, don't eat too much – maybe a small matchbox-sized portion a day. Don't see it as a primary calcium source, more as a vitamin D source.

OILY FISH

Oily fish represents one of the most important groups of foods in a healthy diet. From cardiovascular health to neurological health and everything in between, the health benefits of oily fish are far-reaching. In terms of bone maintenance they are pretty important, from the point of view of general nutritional support. First, they are probably the richest dietary sources of vitamin D. Not many foods contain vitamin D at a significant level if someone is deficient, but oily fish are one of the few that deliver a decent amount of it. Some oily fish, such as sardines and anchovies, are eaten bones and all. The bones in these are a great source of calcium. I recommend eating oily fish three or four times a week.

SEEDS

Seeds make a great snack and are a concentrated source of both calcium and the all-important mineral zinc. A couple of handfuls a day is ideal.

GREENS

Greens are without doubt the kings of magnesium-rich foods. This is due to the element that makes them green – chlorophyll. This substance is very similar to human haemoglobin. It consists of four proteins bound together. In human haemoglobin, each of these protein units has iron bound to it. In chlorophyll the iron is replaced with magnesium. So, the darker and richer the green, the more chlorophyll is in it, which means more magnesium. Fill up on these dietary powerhouses as much as is feasibly possible.

RECEIPES FOR HEALTHY JOINTS
– TOP INGREDIENTS –

The recipes that follow contain ingredients which have medicinal properties that benefit joint health. Here is a rundown of these 'star' ingredients and their medicinal properties:

CELERY (page 144) is an apparently innocuous salad vegetable with a secret weapon hidden up its stringy sleeve. It contains a compound called 3-n-butyphtlalide or NBP for short. This has some analgesic properties. It isn't likely to replace paracetamol any time soon, but it can deliver a short sharp pain killing kick.

GINGER and **TURMERIC** (pages 144, 145, 146, 149, 150) are botanically related; these spices have some very interesting effects upon inflammation. The compounds in turmeric that give it its distinctive bright orange colour, and the compounds in ginger that give it its characteristic spicy flavour, both have been shown to interrupt the production of a type of prostaglandin that

activates inflammation. There are three types of prostaglandin: series 1, series 2 and series 3. Series 1 and 3 are the anti-inflammatory type that are derived from omega 3 fatty acids. Series 2 prostaglandins, on the other hand, activate and exacerbate inflammation. Series 2 are made from a fatty acid called arachidonic acid. The active compounds in turmeric and ginger block the activity of an enzyme called cyclooxygenase that is involved in the conversion of arachidonic acid into series 2 prostaglandins.

SALMON (pages 145, 146, 149), like all oily fish, is a rich source of the omega 3 fatty acids EPA and DHA. These are fed into metabolic pathways that convert them into anti-inflammatory series 1 and 3 prostaglandins. They are also converted into resolvins and protectins that can further reduce inflammation. Long-term increased consumption of these fatty acids has been shown to have significant impact upon numerous inflammatory conditions.

MACKEREL (page 150), like all oily fish, contains omega 3 fatty acids that are vital for the management of any kind of inflammatory condition, especially in the joints. EPA and DHA are metabolised to form anti-inflammatory series 1 and 3 prostaglandins. Many oily fish are also good sources of bioavailable calcium, often better than dairy products.

CAVOLO NERO (page 150) is a very good source of magnesium, calcium and vitamin D; the holy trinity of nutrients for maintaining bone density.

CELERY GINGER JUICE SHOT

SERVES 1

3 sticks celery
2.5cm piece ginger

These simple, spicy morning shots will definitely knock the cobwebs off, not to mention delivering a therapeutic punch.

MEDICINAL PROPERTIES

CELERY

GINGER

Run both ingredients through a juicer to create a small fiery shot of juice.

SPEEDY SALMON CURRY

SERVES 2

½ teaspoon turmeric
½ teaspoon cinnamon
2 salmon fillets
1 large red onion, finely
  chopped
3 cloves garlic, finely chopped
olive oil, for frying
150g red lentils
1 tablespoon Madras curry
  paste
400ml coconut milk
sea salt

MEDICINAL PROPERTIES
SALMON TURMERIC

This is an extremely quick and easy curry. Salmon can be quite tricky to use in a curry, because it flakes apart so easily. This is one way of getting around it.

1. Preheat the oven to 180°C/160°C fan/350°F/gas mark 4. Mix the turmeric and cinnamon and sprinkle them over the salmon fillets, along with a good pinch of salt. Place the fillets on a baking tray and cook for 20 minutes.

2. In a saucepan sauté the onion and garlic with a good pinch of salt in a little olive oil until the onion has softened.

3. Add the lentils, curry paste and coconut milk. Simmer until the lentils have softened, which may take 20–30 minutes. During this time the liquid may reduce a fair bit. Top up with water as necessary, but aim for a porridge-like texture.

4. Put the salmon on plates, then pour the lentil mixture over the top.

SPICED FISH SOUP WITH GINGER AND TURMERIC

SERVES 4

1 large red onion, finely
    chopped
3 cloves garlic, finely chopped
2cm piece ginger, peeled and
    finely chopped
2 stalks lemongrass, bashed
    with a rolling pin to expose
    the fragrant inner
1 small red chilli, finely
    chopped
olive oil, for frying
2 teaspoons turmeric
400g can coconut milk
300ml vegetable stock
2 salmon fillets, diced
150g king prawns
sea salt

This gorgeous soup is a fabulous one-pot wonder. Flavoursome, vibrant and simple. Perfect.

1. In a saucepan, sauté the onion, garlic, ginger, lemongrass and chilli in a little olive oil, along with a good pinch of sea salt, until the onion softens and the lemongrass becomes fragrant.

2. Add the turmeric, coconut milk and vegetable stock, and simmer for about 10–15 minutes, to create a well-flavoured broth.

3. Add the salmon and prawns and simmer for another 8–10 minutes, until the fish has completely cooked. Remove the lemongrass stalks before serving.

MEDICINAL PROPERTIES

GINGER AND TURMERIC
SALMON

SESAME SOY SALMON WITH SPICED BUTTERNUT PURÉE AND PINEAPPLE SALSA

SERVES 2

2 salmon fillets
½ red onion, halved then sliced
1 cloves garlic, finely chopped
1cm piece ginger, peeled and
  finely chopped
olive oil, for frying
¼ butternut squash, skin on,
  diced
150ml vegetable stock
½ teaspoon cinnamon
sea salt

for the salmon marinade
2 tablespoons soy sauce
3 teaspoons honey
1 tablespoon toasted sesame oil

for the pineapple salsa
1 slice fresh pineapple, diced
¼ red onion, very finely chopped
¼ red chilli, thinly sliced
small sprig of coriander, finely
  chopped

MEDICINAL PROPERTIES

GINGER
SALMON

This is a dreamy dish with many flavours and textures hitting you at once.

1. Mix the marinade ingredients together in a bowl. Add the salmon, toss several times and then leave to marinate for a few hours in the fridge.

2. In a saucepan sauté the onion, garlic and ginger in a little olive oil, along with a good pinch of salt, until the onion has softened.

3. Add the squash, together with enough vegetable stock to cover it. Simmer until the squash softens. Add the cinnamon and blend into a smooth purée. Preheat the oven to 180°C/160°C fan/350°F/gas mark 4.

4. Remove the salmon fillets from the marinade and place them on a lined baking tray. Pour a couple of spoonfuls of the marinade over the salmon, and roast for about 20 minutes.

5. While the salmon is roasting, combine all the salsa ingredients.

6. When the salmon is cooked, place a spoonful of the spiced purée in the centre of each serving plate. Place a salmon fillet on top of the purée, and top the salmon with salsa.

7. Serve with some steamed greens.

MISO MACKEREL WITH SPICY KALE

SERVES 2

2 teaspoons miso paste

2 teaspoons honey

1 teaspoon toasted sesame
  oil

2 fresh mackerel fillets

olive oil, for greasing and
  sautéing

2 cloves garlic, finely chopped

1cm piece ginger, peeled and
  grated

½ red chilli, finely chopped

5 handfuls cavolo nero,
  shredded

A beautiful marriage of flavours. Simple and
sumptuous.

1. Combine the miso paste, honey and sesame oil,
and mix well.

2. Preheat the oven to 180°C/160°C fan/350°F/gas mark 4.
Place the mackerel fillets on an oiled baking sheet and
coat with the miso mixture. Bake in the oven for about
20 minutes.

3. In a frying pan sauté the garlic, ginger and chilli in
a little olive oil for a minute or two, then add the cavolo
nero. Sauté for a couple more minutes until the greens
have wilted.

4. Remove the mackerel fillets from the onion and serve
with the vegetables on the side.

MEDICINAL PROPERTIES

CAVOLO NERO
GINGER
MACKEREL

GENERAL TIPS TO REMEMBER FOR HEALTHY JOINTS

While there are some very powerful ingredients that can directly influence joint health, there are also general diet and lifestyle changes that you can make to further support the overall health of the joints. These changes are easy to make and can bring rapid results.

REDUCE ANIMAL PROTEIN INTAKE.
Don't worry, I'm not on a crusade to make everyone eat a specific diet. There is, however, a vast amount of scientific data that shows a correlation between high consumption of animal protein and increased severity of inflammatory conditions. This is usually because animal proteins tend to be high in certain types of fats. If you recall the explanation of prostaglandins – the fat-derived inflammatory regulators – you will remember that some of them are anti-inflammatory, whereas some actually encourage and enhance an inflammatory response. Which ones the body creates is determined by the dietary fats we feed it. Animal fats are the type that the body uses to create the series 2 prostaglandins that worsen inflammatory conditions.

REDUCE REFINED CARBOHYDRATES.
Refined carbs, such as white sugar, white bread, white pasta, white rice and so on, can wreak havoc in the body. All other negative influences aside, refined carbs can adversely affect the immune system and cause our white blood cells to behave rather erratically. It is believed that this can exacerbate some of the inflammatory processes instigated by certain white blood cells. Refined carbohydrates also cause fluctuations in hormones such as insulin, the knock-on effect being increased production of the nasty pro-inflammatory prostaglandins.

THE NERVOUS SYSTEM

The nervous system has to be one of the single most complex systems in the body. Its primary function is to coordinate and regulate activities in the body, and communicate signals and messages between its different parts. It is made up of the brain, spinal cord and the nerves that branch off this and supply all the body's tissues. The nervous system is divided into two distinct parts: the central nervous system (CNS) and the peripheral nervous system (PNS).

The CNS refers to the brain and spinal cord. It can be viewed as being the central computer, where all incoming information is processed, decisions are made and commands are issued. The central nervous system regulates every involuntary action in the body, such as breathing and blinking. The brain is attached to the spinal cord, which branches out many times, dividing into the peripheral nervous system, in order to give nervous supply to all tissues and areas of the body. The spinal cord is, in essence, a thick collected bundle of nerves connecting all aspects of the brain and body.

The peripheral nervous system is the branch of the nervous system that extends beyond the spinal cord and supplies all peripheral tissues. These are the nerves that tell the brain what is going on in the rest of the body and what is happening in our immediate environment.

UNDERSTANDING THE NERVOUS SYSTEM

The better understanding you have of the way the nervous system works, the better you will understand how diet can impact the health of this complex system.

THE NEURON

The neuron or nerve cell is probably the most important when it comes to keeping the nervous system healthy. These specialised cells are designed to carry messages rapidly from the central nervous system out to the peripheries where they instigate action. This happens in a nanosecond, thanks to the structure and function of the neuron. Let's review the different parts that are key to its function.

THE AXON

The axon is the long fibre that runs through the centre of the neuron. Axons transmit information. This could be sensory information, such as touch and taste, or it could be information that causes movement. This is carried along the axon as a rapidly moving electrical impulse called an action potential. The electrical charge races along the axon in a spiralling movement until it reaches the end of the neuron, an area called the terminal.

THE MYELIN SHEATH

The myelin sheath is a dense fatty structure that surrounds the axon. This specialised structure not only offers protection to the axon, but also accelerates the movement of the electrical impulse across the axon.

This acceleration occurs because the sheath is placed along the axon in capsules rather than as a continuous barrier. Imagine it as a string of beads; tiny bits of axon are exposed in the same way as tiny bits of string are exposed between the beads. The electrical impulse jumps between the gaps of exposed axon. These exposed areas are known as nodes of Ranvier. Diet can have a profound effect on keeping the myelin sheath healthy.

TERMINAL AND SYNAPSE

At the ends of the neuron are bulbous, button-like structures called the terminal. Neurons are linked but don't actually touch. There is a gap between them. This is called the synapse. The electrical signals that run along the axon cannot jump this gap. The signal is translated into chemical messengers called neurotransmitters. These chemical messengers are stored in the terminal, and then move out into the gap between the neurons and diffuse into the terminal of the neighbouring neuron, where they are translated back into electrical impulses and sent off on their journey again. Different neurotransmitters instigate different responses and have very different effects.

DIET AND NEUROLOGICAL HEALTH

I'm not going to claim that diet is a magical cure-all for every neurological problem, but the brain and nervous system is a physiological system which has specific nutritional requirements. If these are not met, the consequences are considerable. There are also a few things that diet can help to do.

MAINTAINING THE MYELIN SHEATH

The myelin sheath – the fatty capsular lining of the axon – is in a constant state of flux. It constantly breaks down and builds back up, provided the right building blocks are available. The body uses a very specific essential fatty acid to rebuild and maintain the myelin sheath. This is a member of the omega 3 family called DHA (docosahexaenoic acid). This fatty acid must be obtained from the diet daily. The best source is oily fish. Such fish have DHA preformed in their tissues ready for us to use. The only other dietary source is foods such as nuts and seeds that contain omega 3 in the form of ALA. However, this is where we have a bit of a problem. ALA needs to be converted by enzymes into EPA and DHA – the fatty acids that are used for metabolic and structural purposes. The problem is that our bodies are very bad at this conversion, converting just a couple of per cent. So the first choice is oily fish, where it is found abundantly, or if you don't eat fish, a supplement is the way to go.

REGULATING NEUROTRANSMITTER PRODUCTION AND FUNCTION

As described above, neurotransmitters are the chemicals that carry the signal a nerve sends as an electrical impulse, across the synapse on to the next neuron where it is converted back into an electrical impulse and goes on its way. This is automated, but nutrition supports it. Vitamin B6, for example, is involved in converting the amino acid tryptophan into serotonin. Vitamin B12 is involved in the production of a group of neurotransmitters called monoamines. Other nutrients, such as tryptophan, are the building blocks for neurotransmitters.

KEY FOODS FOR NEUROLOGICAL HEALTH

OILY FISH

Oily fish such as salmon, mackerel, herrings and trout are top of my list for supporting neurological health. This is because they contain high levels of preformed omega 3 fatty acids – EPA and DHA. These are vital both for maintaining the structure of the myelin sheath, and also supporting the structure and function of neurotransmitter receptors, which can improve the release and reception of neurotransmitters. Oily fish are also a good dietary source of vitamin B12.

WHOLEGRAINS

Wholegrains such as brown rice and pearl barley are all very good sources of B vitamins. These play so many roles in the nervous system, from helping us to feel calmer, through to the manufacture of neurotransmitters.

GREEN VEGETABLES

Green vegetables are the best sources of magnesium in the diet. This mineral is involved in more than 1,000 enzymatic reactions and can have a relaxing effect on the central nervous system.

RECIPES FOR A HEATHLY NERVOUS SYSTEM
– TOP INGREDIENTS –

The recipes that follow contain ingredients which have medicinal properties that benefit nerve health. Here is a rundown of these 'star' ingredients and their medicinal properties:

BLUEBERRIES (page 161), along with other dark berries such as blackberries, are rich in a group of compounds called flavonoids. These have been widely studied and found to influence circulation. They are taken up by the endothelial cells that make up the lining of the inner surface of our blood vessels. This makes the endothelial cells secrete nitric oxide, which relaxes the muscular walls of the blood vessels and dilates the vessel. This can lower blood pressure and enhances circulation, especially to the extremities. There is evidence to suggest that enhancing circulation in this way can benefit cognitive function.

BROWN RICE (pages 162, 164) is rich in B vitamins that are vital for the healthy functioning of the nervous system. They regulate many aspects of nerve cell function, not to mention playing an important role in the manufacture of neurotransmitters.

CAVOLO NERO (page 167), like all green vegetables, is extremely rich in the mineral magnesium. This is important in treating anxiety. This is because it helps to relax the nervous system and eases nervous tension. It also relaxes muscle, so can help us to physically feel relaxed. This can be especially important for aiding sleep.

CHOCOLATE (page 168) is not the terrible food that people make it out to be. Cacao, the bean from which chocolate is made, is one of the most nutrient-dense foods on the planet, with more than 1,500 active phytochemicals. Most of us know that something

in chocolate makes us feel better immediately. Well, that isn't just a psychological
effect. There are two amazing compounds
in chocolate that almost instantly affect
our brain chemistry. The first is called anan-
damide. This substance binds to the same
receptors in the brain as the psychoactive
substance THC, found in cannabis. Anan-
damide has some similar properties, in that
it evokes euphoria and also enhances clear
creative thinking. It has been nicknamed the
'bliss molecule'.

The second is a substance called phe-
nylethylamine (PEA). This is another
neurotransmitter that has been linked with
elevation of mood and enhanced focus
and clarity. This chemical is released in the
nervous system when we first fall in love and
have the euphoric feeling that everything is
right with the world.

LAVENDER (page 168) is one of the
best-known plants for mood regulation. The
fragrant oils that give lavender its distinctive
aroma have a very mild but notable sedative
effect upon the nervous system. It helps to
calm and centre the mind, without causing
excessive drowsiness.

MACKEREL (page 162) is a rich source of
the omega 3 fatty acids EPA and DHA that
are essential for neurotransmitter receptor
function and maintaining the health of the
myelin sheath.

OATS (page 161) are a rich source of
B vitamins. These are vital for many aspects
of mental and neurological health. One
of their main roles is in the production of
key neurotransmitters that carry messages
throughout the nervous system. B vitamins
also help to release energy from the food
that we eat. It's difficult to feel in a good
mood or mentally sharp if we are exhausted.
Oats are a low glycaemic choice of grain for
breakfast. They release their sugar content
slowly, rather than flooding the bloodstream
with glucose. This prevents the energy peaks
and troughs associated with eating sugary
and heavily processed cereals that leave us
feeling mentally foggy and make our mood
take a nosedive.

ROSE (page 168) is one of my favourite
herbs for treating any kind of nervous system
issue, especially anxiety and depression. The
compound geraniol has a mild antidepres-
sant effect on the nervous system. It isn't
100 per cent clear why or how this happens,
but it is likely to be a reflex effect that causes
a general relaxation of the central nervous
system.

SALMON (page 163) is packed with omega
3 fatty acids. The fatty acid DHA is a key
component in maintaining the structure of
the neuron, particularly the myelin sheath
that is vital for communication across the
neuron. It is important to have a regular
intake of DHA in order to maintain a healthy
myelin sheath.

SPINACH (page 164) is rich in the mineral magnesium. This vital mineral is involved in more than 1,000 chemical reactions in the body. It is important for everything from energy production to regulating muscular contraction. It can help us to physically relax when we feel anxious and uptight. This is because it is involved in the relaxation of muscle fibres, so it can help us to physically unwind.

STEAK (page 167), enjoyed occasionally, is a very good source of haem iron. There is a huge link between very low levels of iron and anxiety and depression. This is especially true for women who experience iron loss during menstruation.

COCONUT PORRIDGE WITH BERRY GINGER COMPOTE

SERVES 1

80g porridge oats
400ml coconut milk

for the compote
180g blueberries
2.5cm piece ginger,
  peeled and grated

MEDICINAL PROPERTIES

BLUEBERRIES
OATS

This simple breakfast is a cocktail of nutrients that support the health of the nervous system, and it will keep you full until lunch.

1. Put the berries and ginger in a saucepan with a tablespoon of water. Bring to the boil and simmer for about 20 minutes until it has a jam-like texture. Allow to cool.

2. Put the oats and coconut milk in another saucepan, bring to the boil and simmer for 3–4 minutes. Add water if desired to achieve your preferred texture.

3. Pour the porridge into a bowl and spoone the compote into the centre of it.

MACKEREL KEDGEREE

SERVES 2

1 large red onion, finely
   chopped
1 clove garlic, finely chopped
olive oil, for frying
½ teaspoon ground coriander
½ teaspoon turmeric
1 teaspoon curry powder
150g brown basmati rice
300ml vegetable stock
2 smoked mackerel fillets
2 eggs, hard boiled
sea salt

MEDICINAL PROPERTIES

BROWN RICE
MACKEREL

This slight twist on a classic tastes wonderful and makes a superb weekend brunch.

1. In a saucepan, sauté the onion and garlic in a little olive oil, along with a good pinch of salt, until the onion has softened.

2. Add the coriander, turmeric, curry powder and rice, and then the vegetable stock. Bring to the boil, then reduce to a simmer, cover and cook for 10 minutes.

3. Remove the lid, take the pan off the heat and allow to stand for 10–15 minutes.

4. Divide the rice between two plates. Flake the mackerel over the top. Slice the eggs into quarters and divide between the plates.

WASABI SALMON WITH GINGERED GREENS

SERVES 2

1 teaspoon wasabi paste
2 teaspoons honey
2 teaspoons soy sauce
2 salmon fillets
5 handfuls curly kale,
  shredded
2.5cm piece ginger, peeled
  and grated
olive oil, for frying

This is one of my favourite dishes, and it is extremely easy to make.

1. In a small bowl mix the wasabi, honey and soy sauce.

2. Preheat the oven to 180°C/160°C fan/350°F/gas mark 4. Put the salmon fillets on a baking tray, and top with the wasabi mixture. Bake in the oven for about 20 minutes.

3. In a frying pan sauté the kale and ginger in a little olive oil for 2–3 minutes, until the kale has wilted. Plate the kale up and serve the salmon on top.

MEDICINAL PROPERTIES

SALMON

BROWN RICE BIBIMBAP

SERVES 2

150g short grain brown rice
6 shiitake mushrooms, sliced
olive oil, for frying
2 large handfuls baby spinach
2 eggs
1 carrot, grated
2 tablespoons sesame oil
2 tablespoons gochujang
  (Korean hot chilli paste)

MEDICINAL PROPERTIES

BROWN RICE
SPINACH

I absolutely adore Korean food, and bibimbap is at the top of the list for me. There are many variations, but the vegetarian version definitely wins. Swapping traditional white rice for brown increases the nutrients and reduces the glycaemic impact. Korean chilli paste can be found in Asian supermarkets or online.

1. Place the rice in a saucepan, cover with boiling water and simmer over a low heat for 30 minutes, or until soft and fully cooked.

2. In a frying pan sauté the mushrooms in a little olive oil, until cooked.

3. Remove the mushrooms and sauté the spinach in a little olive oil until wilted.

4. Fry the eggs in a separate pan in a little olive oil, sunny side up.

5. Divide the cooked rice between two deep bowls and add the spinach, mushrooms and grated carrot. Top each with a fried egg.

6. Add a tablespoon of chilli paste and a tablespoon of sesame oil to each bowl, and mix, allowing the egg yolk to seep through.

SURF AND TURF

SERVES 2

1 clove garlic, finely chopped
olive oil, for frying
3 handfuls cavolo nero,
  shredded
2 sirloin steaks
8 raw king or tiger prawns
2 tablespoons garlic butter
sea salt and cracked black
  pepper

MEDICINAL PROPERTIES

CAVOLO NERO
STEAK

This awesome dish is a healthier version of the old steak house classic. I don't recommend eating red meat often, but for non-vegetarians, there are very few sources of iron as great as red meat.

1. In a frying pan sauté the garlic in a little olive oil, along with a pinch of salt. Add the shredded cavolo nero and continue to sauté until wilted.

2. Season the steaks with salt and a little black pepper, and cook according to your preference.

3. In a separate pan, sauté the prawns in the garlic butter for 4–5 minutes, until fully pink, turning occasionally.

4. Place the greens in the centre of each serving plate. Top them with a steak, then top each steak with four prawns, and spoon any remaining garlic butter over them.

LAVENDER AND ROSE CHOCOLATE

MAKES ABOUT 10
(Depending on size of
your moulds)

100g dark chocolate (70 per
   cent cocoa)
½ teaspoon lavender flowers
5 drops lavender essential oil
6 teaspoon rose water

MEDICINAL PROPERTIES

CHOCOLATE
LAVENDER
ROSE

This recipe is absolutely divine. It's not often that
a health-related book encourages the consumption
of chocolate, but this is one of those rare exceptions.
This bar takes the powerful mood-enhancing
properties of chocolate to the next dimension.

1. Break the chocolate into small pieces and place in
a heatproof glass bowl. Place the bowl over a pan of
gently simmering water to create a bain-marie. Allow
the chocolate to melt.

2. Add the lavender flowers and the two essential oils.
Mix well, and then transfer to the moulds of your choice.
You could make a single bar, or small bite-size pieces.
I tend to use an ice-cube mould, so I have little bite-size
pieces to nibble when I feel like a fix.

GENERAL TIPS TO REMEMBER FOR NERVOUS SYSTEM HEALTH

TAKE TIME OUT. If you feel as if everything is starting to get on top of you, it's time to take a break – even if that's a five-minute walk round the block or ten minutes of meditation or focused relaxation. Our nervous system has the capacity to withstand a huge amount, provided we give it the chance to recover. Continual stress and emotional upset can lead us to a state of nervous exhaustion, which can result in burnout and even the onset of depression. Finding your own ways to cope with what life throws at you can be a lifesaver.

REDUCE ALCOHOL INTAKE. Alcohol can only bring you down. Even though it can bring on the giggles, it is a natural depressant. It affects brain chemistry in such a way that our 'feel good' neurotransmitters, such as serotonin, become depleted.

KEEP BLOOD SUGAR EVEN. Blood sugar can have a huge impact on both our mood and how we respond to stress. When we consume foods that send our blood sugar levels up too quickly, it throws our whole hormonal system out of balance. We produce huge surges of insulin to deal with the sudden rise in sugar. This disrupts the production and levels of other hormones throughout the body and can lead to very low mood and a feeling of being overwhelmed by the most minor situation.

NATURE'S EDIBLE PHARMACY

This section of the book is a simple A–Z guide to the most powerful common medicinal foods on the planet. The focus of this book is foods that are powerful for reasons that stretch beyond the scope of mere nutrition. The foods included are those which possess some powerful phytochemicals that make the foods more than just sources of fuel and nutrients, so they become medicines in their own right. I have included a break-down of the phytochemical content and medicinal properties for each food, plus some suggestions as to how they may be used. Get in that kitchen, get creative and cook yourself a cure!

FRUIT

Fruit has to be a gift from the gods, and is the single most important food for human beings. Do you think it is a coincidence that nature designed fruits to be so attractive to virtually all our senses? Their colours are bright and vibrant. Their aromas are lingering and their flavours are sweet and sensuous. They are our number one food. Fruits are rich in antioxidants, minerals and many of the water-soluble vitamins. They provide huge amounts of fibre and sustained energy and require virtually no energy or effort to digest. Many fruits are also powerful medicines. Gone are the days when your medicine needed to taste awful. Make the most of nature's most divine medicine.

APPLES

We are all familiar with the age-old saying, 'An apple a day keeps the doctor away.' How true that is! They are such a simple every-day staple that we really do take them for granted. Simple though they may be, apples are a wonderful medicine.

One of the most important compounds in apples is a soluble fibre called pectin. Those of you who make your own jam may be familiar with pectin. It forms a gelatinous texture, helping jam to set. In the body, pectin has the ability to chemically bind to LDL cholesterol and carry it out of the body via the digestive tract. Pectin is also known to support digestive transit, as it swells in the digestive tract, increasing bulk of the stool and making it softer and easier to pass.

Apples have gained a strong reputation as a useful remedy for preventing asthma attacks. This folk remedy has now been backed up by a small degree of scientific study. Almost every variety of apple con-

tains significant levels of a flavonoid called phloridzin, which is known to help reduce localised inflammation of the bronchioles. Asthma is an immune-mediated reactive inflammation of the bronchioles, so any natural protection against this reaction is certainly going to improve the condition. OK, it may be tenuous, but interesting nonetheless.

The final compound found in quite high levels in apples is a powerful chemical called ellagic acid. This magical antioxidant compound is known to be a powerful antimutagenic. This means that it is able to reduce the ability of potentially carcinogenic substances to initiate cancerous changes in a cell's DNA. When certain environmental influences bind to a cell, or gain entry to a cell, they have the potential to change the genetic material within the cell's DNA, and that can lead to a sudden out-of-control cellular division that can be the start of a tumour.

★ BEST WAY TO USE

In general, I would say eat whole and fresh. In some circumstances apples can be cooked. Cooking destroys some of the antioxidants, but retains the pectin.

BANANAS

One of the most widely consumed foods on the planet, the humble banana is more than just a sweet treat. Bananas are famous for their amazingly high levels of the mineral potassium. This makes them an ideal food for the health of the cardiovascular system. This is because potassium is key in regulating heart rhythm and levels of body fluids. If levels of potassium are slightly higher than sodium, for example, our body will hold on to a lot less fluid. This is beneficial for our blood pressure, because the more fluid the body holds on to, the more blood volume increases. As blood volume increases, simple physics tells us that the pressure within the vessels will also increase.

Bananas also contain a very sticky, soothing carbohydrate that has been traditionally used as a remedy for issues such as gastritis. It seems to soothe inflamed surfaces within the gastrointestinal tract.

★ BEST WAY TO USE

They can be eaten whole, or mashed with a little honey and mixed seeds. Yum!

BLUEBERRIES

These luscious, purple little treats are one of the kings of the fruit domain, although they have acquired an almost mythical reputation. The most noteworthy property of blueberries is their super-high antioxidant content. The vivid blue/purple pigment found in blueberry skins is derived from a group of chemicals called anthocyanidins, the same family of chemicals that is found in grapes and red wine. Anthocyanidins are antioxidants first and foremost. This means that they help to protect tissues against oxidative damage. This is the kind of damage caused by normal metabolic reactions to energy production, associated with almost every disease at some level or another, from normal ageing through to the initiation of cancer and heart disease. It is for this reason that high consumption of foods rich in antioxidants is associated with a reduced incidence of such diseases.

Blueberries are widely studied for cardiovascular benefits because of the high levels of flavonoids they contain. These substances move into the endothelial cells that line blood vessels and cause them to secrete a substance called nitric oxide. This causes relaxation of the muscular walls that make up the bulk of blood vessels. When these muscles relax, the vessel widens and the pressure within it drops. Hence regular consumption of flavonoid-rich foods can help reduce blood pressure and improve endothelial function.

★ BEST WAY TO USE

Eaten with a little yoghurt. The fats in the yoghurt increase the absorption of the antioxidant chemicals.

CHERRIES

These delicious treats are one of my favourite fruits. The rich, juicy flesh is bursting with antioxidants. The darker the cherries the better, as the darker colour represents higher levels of antioxidants.

Cherries are most famously used as a remedy for gout. This painful condition arises from crystals of uric acid forming in the joints. This allows spikes of uric acid crystal to press into surrounding soft tissues in the joint, which causes pain and triggers inflammation. Cherries contain a type of anthocyanidin (a similar chemical to that found in red wine), unique to this fruit, which has been shown to inhibit a substance called xanthine oxidase, which is the enzyme the body uses to manufacture uric acid. Inhibiting this enzyme will cause uric acid levels in the body to drop, and reduce the likelihood of an excess starting to crystallise in the joints.

★ BEST WAY TO USE

Eaten fresh, ideally, although it can also be consumed as juice.

CRANBERRIES

Cranberries are synonymous with Christmas dinner, Thanksgiving or a good Sunday roast. A close cousin to the blueberry, cranberries have a similarly high antioxidant level, which comes from their deep red pigment.

In traditional medicine, cranberries are noted for their protection against urinary tract infections. This is due to the presence of compounds called proanthocyanidins. These powerful antioxidants stop bacteria such as *E. coli* from adhering to the inner wall of the urinary tract. The bacteria attach to the inner lining of the urinary tract to cause infection, stimulating the immune system to respond with inflammation. This leads to discomfort and the classic symptoms of painful urination and urinary urgency. Preventing the bacteria adhering stops the infection. The proanthocyanidins can also pluck them off the urinary tract walls if infection has already set in, thus shortening the duration of infection.

★ BEST WAY TO USE

I personally think that nothing beats eating them fresh. They are quite sour and best mixed with a little yoghurt. If you find the fresh berries disagreeable, then consuming the juice is OK, although definitely second place in my view.

DATES

I absolutely love dates (not just the dinner and flowers kind). They are like sweets to me. One of my favourite snacks to satisfy a sweet craving is dates dipped in a little organic peanut butter.

Dates are a rich source of a special, large and complex sugar called beta glucan. This incredible sugar has some profound health benefits. First, it has a reputation for removing LDL cholesterol from the body. It does this by chemically binding with it, rendering it inactive, and enabling it to be carried out of the body. The second, and probably most profound, effect of beta glucan is its ability to influence the immune system. It has been shown to cause a systemic rise in white blood cell numbers. Beta glucan can indirectly cause the body to manufacture more white blood cells, and make them act in a more aggressive manner. This effect has most famously been demonstrated with medicinal mushrooms such as shiitake, maitake and reishi. The beta glucans in these mushrooms are the most biologically active and aggressive, but foods such as dates also stimulate this activity to a lesser degree.

★ BEST WAY TO USE

I eat them just as they are or add them to baked food such as flapjacks.

GRAPES

Grapes have always been associated with health and recovery. They seem to be the staple food taken into hospitals as a gift for sick friends and loved ones.

Grapes (the red and purple varieties) have a reputation as a tool for protecting and maintaining heart health, especially in their fermented form (vino of course!). They contain a chemical pigment called anthocyanidins. These are part of the red/purple pigments in the grapes. These compounds are known to reduce the oxidisation of LDL cholesterol, thus preventing arterial damage. It isn't cholesterol itself that damages the circulatory system, rather the body oxidising the cholesterol, which then causes inflammation and in turn causes damage to the lining of the arteries, leading to blood clot formation.

Anthocyanidins have also been shown to cause notable relaxation of the muscles that line the blood vessel walls. In doing so, they allow the blood vessel walls to widen, thus increasing their internal space. Simple physics tells us that if the contents of the vessel (i.e. blood volume) stay the same, but the size of the vessel increases, the pressure within it will go down.

Grapes contain another compound believed to be linked to their cardioprotective properties. That is the antioxidant compound resveratrol. This compound is known to reduce the build-up of plaques within the artery walls, thus minimising the risk of vascular injury and the inevitable clot formation that follows. Resveratrol is also reputed to be an anti-ageing ingredient for the skin. Best rely on whole, raw grapes for this, rather than red wine. As with all things in life, there is always a trade-off. There would be little point in having lovely wrinkle-free skin, if that was accompanied by a bright red boozer's nose and eye bags that made Miss Piggy look like a beauty queen!

★ BEST WAY TO USE

A glass of a good quality red wine with a meal is one of my ideas of heaven. Once you drink more than one or two glasses a day, the protective properties are cancelled out by damage and irritation to the liver and upper digestive tract. So be sensible. The best way is eat the grapes whole and fresh. But I guess we all need a little fun.

LEMONS AND LIMES

I have included these two fruits together, as apart from a couple of tiny insignificant chemicals, they are virtually identical.

Limes are actually responsible for the discovery of vitamin C. When British sailors went to sea on long journeys, most ended up suffering from scurvy. Expeditions that carried limes for sailors to consume, on the other hand, did not. This eventually led to the discovery of vitamin C, and to Brits earning the unfortunate nickname of limeys!

Both lemons and limes have a very high concentration of a compound called kaempferol. This substance is known to be a powerful protective agent against cancer, as it reduces uncontrolled cell division. It seems most protective – at least from an epidemiological perspective – against breast cancer. Kaempferol is also a potent antibiotic agent. This was first demonstrated in village populations in West Africa, where there were frequent and aggressive cholera outbreaks. Lime juice was added to the villagers' staple rice-based dish, and episodes of cholera began to decline. This led to further investigation that revealed that kaempferol was the magic bullet in this case.

Lemons and limes offer further protection from cancer thanks to the presence of a powerful phytochemical called limonin. Limonin is believed to be chemoprotective. This means that it is able to defend cells against the damaging effects of carcinogens. Carcinogens are chemical compounds, both natural metabolic by-products and environmental chemicals, that can cause damage to a cell's DNA, which may then lead to an unnatural division and cancerous changes of the cell.

★ BEST WAY TO USE

Add fresh lemon or lime juice to salad dressings, dips, sauces or to hot water.

MANGO

Mangoes are one of my favourite fruits. I'm eating an ice-cold one from the fridge as I write this. They are sweet, aromatic and so very exotic.

Apart from being very high in the antioxidant compound beta-carotene, they are also a useful digestive aid. Similar to papayas, mangoes contain some highly active enzymes that are beneficial in the correct digestion of proteins. These enzymes are so powerful that mango is sometimes used as a meat tenderiser.

★ BEST WAY TO USE

Eaten fresh, or blended with natural yoghurt and a little water to make a refreshing mango lassi.

PAPAYA

Papaya is a very delicious sweet fruit – not one of my favourites, but it certainly satisfies the sweet craving from time to time.

Papaya contains some powerful enzymes. The best known of these is a compound called papain. This is a protein-digesting enzyme. I often recommend papaya, or an extract of papain, to individuals who have had long-standing illness or are weak and need building up, as it increases their protein digestion and absorption.

Papain is also commonly used for allergies, especially hay fever. This is because it is believed to be an effective natural antihistamine. Allergic reactions such as hay fever cause a localised histamine release that is responsible for most of the inflammation and symptoms associated with such conditions. Anything that affects the levels of histamine produced can have a notable effect upon the severity of such conditions.

★ BEST WAY TO USE

Eaten raw, juiced or taken as an extract.

PINEAPPLE

One of my favourite fruits. Pineapples conjure up images of white sandy beaches and grass skirts. Maybe that's just me! But their exotic flavour and aroma is certainly comforting on some level.

Pineapples contain a powerful enzyme called bromelain. This wonderful compound is great for enhancing protein digestion, but its medicinal properties are far more profound than that. Bromelain is a powerful anti-inflammatory. It can rapidly and efficiently soften swollen tissues, and ease them back to normal functioning. I find pineapple to be a very useful food for arthritics and those with inflammation of the digestive tract.

★ BEST WAY TO USE

I tend to juice pineapple. It is also great in smoothies. The most important thing to note, however you choose to eat it, is to ensure that you do not discard the slightly tougher inner core of the pineapple. This contains the highest concentration of bromelain.

GRAINS

Virtually every culture has grains at the forefront of its diet: rice in Asia, maize in Africa and South America, and wheat in Europe and North America. These staple foods can at once be some of the most health-promoting foods, and also the most detrimental to our health. The problem arose when we began refining grains, which mostly involves the removal of the outer coating of the grain. This is the difference between white rice and brown rice, for example: brown has the outer husk, and white doesn't.

The refining of grains creates some significant problems. First, much of the nutrition and phytochemistry is in the outer husk. This means that the refined grains are essentially supplying dead calories, and in cultures where these foods are a dietary staple, it also means that a population can become deficient in important nutrients.

The second, and in my opinion most significant, issue that arises from refining foods is the impact that they have on our blood sugar. When the grains are in their original (whole) state, they release their sugars into the bloodstream at a very slow rate. This gives us a stable energy level. However, when the grains are refined, they cause a sudden and very sharp rise in blood sugar levels. This makes the body release a large amount of insulin (the hormone that regulates the amount of sugar in our bloodstream), in order to deal with the sudden rise in blood sugar. Insulin forces the body's cells to 'suck in' the sugar as quickly as possible, to get it out of the bloodstream. However, the cells can only take in so much sugar at one time and very often when consuming refined carbohydrates, there is still an excess in circulation. When this happens, the body turns the excess sugar into fat, so it can be stored to get it out of the way.

Refined carbohydrate consumption has been directly linked to diseases such as heart disease, cancer, type 2 diabetes and obesity. I believe that our consumption of them is one of the most significant contributing factors to the increase in disease in our modern times.

AMARANTH

Amaranth is not widely known in the Western world. It is a tiny grain that was once a staple food for the Aztecs.

Apart from being a gluten-free grain, rich in protein and every conceivable mineral on Earth, amaranth has a track record as an effective astringent, useful in treating digestive problems such as excessive diarrhoea. Astringents are plants that help to 'dry out' secretory surfaces – such as those that line the gut. They do this by irritating those surfaces, causing them to release proteins that develop a lining on such surfaces, preventing their secretory action. In the context of diarrhoea, the astringent action of amaranth stops too much water entering the digestive tract too rapidly, so helps to give more bulk and texture to the stool.

The most interesting effect of amaranth, however, is its impact upon cholesterol. Something in this grain, yet to be identified, increases the liver's production of an enzyme called 7-alpha-hydroxylase. This is the enzyme that the liver uses to break down cholesterol into bile acids, which can then be easily excreted via the bowel.

★ BEST WAY TO USE

As a replacement for rice. Boil until soft.

BROWN RICE

A staple food, rice prepared in the right way can be one of the most health-giving foods there is. I remember a time in Japan when I ate brown rice at least twice a day and my energy levels and digestion were fantastic, and my appetite sustained.

Brown rice is rich in a whole host of compounds that can help to lower cholesterol. These range from simple dietary fibres through to a compound called gamma oryzanol, which is known to reduce the production of LDL cholesterol.

Brown rice also contains a large number of a group of antioxidant compounds called polyphenols. These antioxidant phytochemicals help to protect the inner lining of the blood vessels against damage.

Apart from this, the high fibre content of brown rice makes it a wonderful food for diabetics. This is because it is a very slow release sugar food. Its fibre also slows down the release of the sugars from other foods consumed with it. This means that the meal will not cause rapid rises in blood sugar or the inevitable insulin spike that follows.

★ BEST WAY TO USE

I use brown rice with curries and the usual dishes that would suit a rice accompaniment. It is also possible to use rice flour to make gluten-free pasta and bread.

BUCKWHEAT

Buckwheat is another grain that is becoming more popular. Eaten widely in Asian countries such as Japan, it is often ground into a flour to make noodles and pastas.

Buckwheat is very high in a group of antioxidant compounds called flavonoids. Two really stand out: rutin and quercetin. In clinical trials rutin has been shown to offer significant protection against damage to the inner lining of blood vessels and clot formation. Quercetin, on the other hand, is an incredibly powerful compound that is useful against allergies. During the allergic response, certain white blood cells release a chemical called histamine, which causes many of the symptoms of hay fever. Quercetin somehow inhibits the release of histamine at this local level, so can offer significant improvement to some allergic reactions.

Both rutin and quercetin have also been associated with a reduction in platelet aggregation. This means they play a role in protecting against excessive blood clotting, helping prevent heart attacks and strokes.

★ BEST WAY TO USE

Buckwheat grains are fantastic toasted and eaten as breakfast cereals. Their most commonly eaten form is soba noodles, which are heavenly stir-fried with vegetables or served cold with a soy and wasabi dip.

OATS

Oats are among the most widely consumed grains in the world. They are a breakfast staple in Europe and the US, and have been associated with health for decades. But what exactly is so special about them? Oats contain a soluble fibre known as beta glucan. This complex sugar forms a gelatinous texture in the digestive tract which allows it to bind to LDL cholesterol and carry it out of the digestive tract so it is not absorbed into the bloodstream.

Beta glucan also has an interesting influence on the immune system. It has been shown in numerous trials to stimulate the production of a group of immune cells called natural killer cells. It does this by interacting with patches of tissue in the gut wall called Peyer's patches. These patches are like surveillance stations, watching what is happening inside the gut. They contain a lot of immune cells that tell the rest of the immune system what to do if an invader makes its way into the body via the gut. The cells do this by sending chemical messengers throughout the body to recruit the correct type of immune cells to combat the invader they have come across. Beta glucan fools the cells in the Peyer's patches that the body is under a specific type of bacterial attack, so they encourage the production of more white blood cells. This can strengthen the immune system in times of infection and stress. It is beta glucan that makes medicinal mushrooms such as shiitake and maitake such powerhouses.

★ BEST WAY TO USE

Few things are more comforting than a bowl of warm porridge on a winter's morning. This is one of the best ways to serve oats, as the heat encourages the release of the beta glucan (this is what makes it thick and gloopy). I always advise making porridge with water rather than milk, as the proteins in milk can bind to the beta glucan and hinder its absorption by the body.

NUTS AND SEEDS

There has been an upward trend in the consumption of nuts and seeds in recent years. Fifteen years ago, the only contact most of us had with these foods was when the odd one turned up in a cereal bar or breakfast muesli, or the scattering of sesame seeds on the top of a burger bun! In the last few years, however, countless nutrition and lifestyle books, health experts and press articles have enlightened us as to the nutritional power of these foods. Beyond their nutritional profile as a rich source of omega 3 and 6 fatty acids, plus a few minerals, some nuts and seeds have some pretty powerful medicinal phytochemicals too!

BRAZIL NUTS

Brazil nuts are one of my absolute favourites; I love their luscious creamy flavour. These nuts aren't high in any exotic phytochemicals, but they're exceptionally high in the trace mineral selenium, which helps the body to produce its own natural antioxidant enzyme, called glutathione peroxidase. This helps in the breakdown and clearance of waste products from the body, and helps regulate the activity of certain groups of white blood cells. This can improve immune function, particularly in inflammatory conditions.

 BEST WAY TO USE

I love to make a nut pâté out of them, or include them in veggie burgers – or just munch them straight from the bag.

COCONUT

Yes, that's right – it's a nut. Coconut has some wonderful nutritional and medicinal properties. The water within coconuts is the best isotonic drink on the planet. It contains a perfect balance of the electrolytes used by our body – sodium, calcium, potassium and magnesium. It can rehydrate us in minutes.

Coconuts also contain a unique type of fat, called medium chain triglycerides (MCTs), which are believed to aid weight loss, due to their ability to force dietary fats to be burned as energy, rather than stored. On a personal note, I always get a little suspicious when I hear 'miracle' weight loss claims, so for me, the jury is still out.

Coconuts contain a compound called lauric acid, which appears to offer considerable potential benefits as an antiviral agent. When we take in a source of lauric acid, the body converts it into a substance called monolaurin. This compound can be protective against all manner of viruses. It works by breaking down certain structures on the outside of fatty coated viruses. In particular, it attacks the structures that viruses use to attach to and enter our cells. Without this ability, the viruses cannot cause infection, cannot replicate and quickly die out.

Coconut is also very high in another acid called caprylic acid. This is one of the best things for dealing with *Candida* infection of the digestive tract. Caprylic acid can kill *Candida* almost on contact.

★ BEST WAY TO USE

I use the oil in dishes almost every day. It is good in curries and sweet dishes because of its wonderful flavour. Coconut milk is also a great addition to smoothies, and coconut flesh is wonderful in desserts and sweet, raw food recipes.

FLAX SEEDS (LINSEED)

Flaxseeds are one of the staple features of any health food shop shelf. Traditionally, flax has been used as a gentle laxative as it has a semi soluble outer coating that forms a gelatinous mass, which can help 'move things along' a little.

Flaxseeds contain a group of compounds called plant lignans. Lignans are a type of fibre that is known to bind to oestrogen receptors on the surfaces of cells. This binding is believed to offer protection against some hormone dependent cancers such as breast cancer. Lignans also help to break down and remove oestrogen from the body by increasing the production of chemicals that facilitate this.

★ BEST WAY TO USE

On cereals, in smoothies, in crackers and breads – or taken in a small glass of water.

PUMPKIN SEEDS

These seemingly ordinary little seeds are actually medicinal powerhouses. I love them.

Pumpkin seeds have long been known as a perfect food for prostate health. This is because they contain a compound called beta sitosterol, which helps to inhibit normal testosterone turning into its evil twin – dihydrotestosterone. Normal testosterone is conducive to overall health and normal functioning of the prostate. However, certain circumstances can cause this healthy testosterone to turn into an aggressively mischievous version called dihydrotestosterone. This can cause enlargement of the prostate, which can be the starting point for prostatic cancer.

Beta sitosterol is also highly beneficial to heart health. This is because it helps to reduce cholesterol. You may well be aware of the myriad drinks and spreads, loaded with 'plant sterols', that reduce cholesterol. Beta sitosterol is one of the most powerful of the plant sterols. Essentially, these compounds help to block the absorption of cholesterol in the intestines. When the liver manufactures cholesterol, a large proportion is released into the intestine from the liver. Here it is reabsorbed back into the bloodstream where it can do its work. Blocking this intestinal absorption has been shown to notably reduce blood cholesterol levels.

Pumpkin seeds also contain another powerful chemical called cucurbitin. Cucurbitin is a major constituent in these seeds and has been shown to have a very powerful anti-parasitic effect in many test tube studies. This gives pumpkin seeds the potential to be used as remedies against such digestive issues as *Candida*, and maybe as an adjunct in the treatment of food poisoning.

★ BEST WAY TO USE

Raw, roasted, eaten straight from the bag or made into a 'butter', I'll eat them any way they come.

CULINARY HERBS AND SPICES

Many of us today are becoming increasingly familiar with the huge array of exotic spices and aromatic herbs that the world has to offer. Our love of fancy food and exotic flavours has led us along a path of culinary discovery as far as they are concerned. Many of us don't realise that they are, in fact, some of the most powerful medicinal compounds on Earth. Some are as strong as pharmaceutical drugs, and all of them are immeasurably safer. So revered were many of these herbs and spices in the past that they were used as a form of currency in some ancient cultures – particularly in ancient Greece and Egypt. Herbs and spices have been a focal part of traditional medicinal systems for millennia. The Ayurvedic traditional medicine system of India, based on more than 5,000 years of wisdom, makes full use of the many exotic spices found on India's shores. Likewise Thai traditional medicine, in which many culinary recipes double as folk remedies for ailments. Traditional Chinese medicine also uses many common culinary herbs as medicines and ingredients for traditional herbal preparations.

For some illogical reason, modern Western society now views medicinal herbs and spices as some kind of New Age hogwash, that while sounding nice have no substance or scientific grounding. Nothing could be further from the truth. The chemistry of aromatic plants is among some of the most complex and highly active in nature. They are the strongest medicines of all plants. The substances that deliver their enticing smells and exotic flavours can have all kinds of amazing interactions with our body tissues and systems. Some are powerful antibiotics, some are painkillers and others can tackle inflammation.

This section will take you through these amazing plants one by one and demonstrate just how effective they are, not to mention giving you some inspiration to get into the kitchen and be creative with nature's most powerful and pleasant medicines.

ANISEED

This sweet and aromatic spice is recognisable to almost everyone, and has been a sweetshop favourite for centuries. In the same family as celery, fennel, dill and carrots, aniseed has been used in traditional remedies in Europe since the fourteenth century in many countries. The fragrant oil anethol, the substance with the instantly recognisable smell, is responsible for the medicinal actions of this plant. Once ingested the oil relaxes the smooth muscle surfaces it comes into contact with. Smooth muscle makes up the walls of tissues such as blood vessels and the digestive tract. This muscle is laid down in several layers that run in differing directions, so that when they contract or relax, they alter the shape and diameter of the organ that they are in. This contraction and relaxation regulates the normal functioning of the organ in question. Ingesting plants that have an effect on this musculature can manipulate normal functioning to give a therapeutic effect.

Aniseed is traditionally used in tea form as an antispasmodic for the intestines. It can relieve the strong, spasm-like pain associated with conditions such as IBS and colic. The wonderful fragrant essential oils are able to relax the smooth muscle of the intestinal walls, thus easing excessive spasms – which are a more forceful and rapid manifestation of our normal intestinal contractions, peristalsis. Aniseed is also considered an effective carminative. This means that it can disperse gas within the digestive system, making it an excellent remedy for bloating and digestive discomfort, and especially useful for infant colic, *Candida* infection and IBS.

Aniseed has been used as a traditional cough remedy. It was infused in spirits or wine to make a tonic liquor called anisette. This remedy was thought to open up the small tubes (bronchioles) of the lungs and ease bronchitis and asthma. If the bronchioles are dilated and widened, it makes it easier to cough up or move phlegm, not to mention increasing airflow. The seed was also ground and used in lozenges to ease mild coughs. These allow the herb to gently coat the area and act for longer.

★ BEST WAY TO USE

For digestive complaints, tea or any kind of water infusion is the best method for rapid results. I would recommend 2–3 teaspoons of seeds, gently crushed with the back of a spoon, per person, per cup. For coughs and catarrh, a home-made anisette would be the best preparation.

BASIL

This vibrant green staple of Italian cuisine is familiar to us all, and is one of the easiest home remedies to obtain or grow. It is also one of the easiest to use, as it can be added directly to your food in a million and one different ways. Used as medicine all over the world, basil has a history of use in traditional Chinese medicine spanning more than 3,000 years. It has probably been used in European medicine for a similar length of time.

Being in the same family as mint, basil shares some of the same properties. So basil is a useful remedy for bloating, digestive cramps, flatulence and colic. As with many fragrant spices, the potent fragrant oils have a relaxing effect on the musculature of the intestinal wall, easing cramps and spasms.

Basil is also an effective anxiolytic (calms anxiety) and sedative, so is a tasty stress-relief aid. Many traditional texts recommend basil tea for mild depression and melancholy. This traditional application, however, is not well supported in modern herbal literature, so its effectiveness remains unclear.

The thing about basil that interests me the most is its anthelmintic/vermifuge activity. These old medical terms refer to the ability to rid the body of parasites such as yeasts and worms. In today's high consumption of convenience foods and high sugar intake, the presence of parasites, particularly yeasts such as *Candida albicans*, is a very common problem. It is therefore reassuring that there are foodstuffs that we can consume (along with getting our diet right in the first place) to aid our body's defence against these troublesome parasites. Again, the powerful essential oils in basil are believed to be responsible for this, as they can be toxic to more simple organisms, killing them rapidly. The key to this action is to make sure that the foodstuff is not cooked so as to give maximum effect.

★ **BEST WAY TO USE**

The good thing about basil is its versatility. It can be used in so many dishes. For maximum effect I recommend that you use it raw where possible, to preserve its essential oils.

CARDAMOM

This is one of my favourite medicinal spices. Hailing from India, its beautiful flavour and aroma lend themselves well to both sweet and savoury dishes, not to mention traditional herbal preparations.

Cardamom is commonly used as a digestive aid in many traditional medical systems, again due to the presence of some powerful fragrant essential oils that have the properties outlined above, making it another remedy to consider for digestive complaints such as nausea, bloating and digestive cramps.

★ BEST WAY TO USE

Cardamom is amazing in teas or used in desserts. My favourite tea is cardamom, skullcap, lavender and rose.

CHILLI

This powerful fiery spice that gives curries their heat has been used in almost every culture in one way or another for both culinary and medicinal purposes. It is a very versatile medicine, affecting many body systems and physical conditions.

One of the major applications of chilli is as a cardiovascular tonic to enhance circulation. The powerful chemical capsaicin, that gives chilli its fiery flavour, has a potent effect on the musculature of artery walls. In short, it almost forces a relaxation of the arterial walls by irritating the smooth muscle, causing it to suddenly relax, thus widening the blood vessels and enhancing circulation – especially to the peripheries (fingers, toes and brain). Another positive consequence of this action is that blood pressure is lowered – the vessel has widened, so its internal diameter increases, putting less pressure on the vessel wall, lessening the likelihood of injury.

Chilli is also a renowned painkiller when used topically (on the skin). When applied to a painful area, it has an instant initial irritating effect on the nerve endings of surrounding tissues. This increases the release of the pain-signalling chemical known as substance P. Now, it may sound somewhat counter-intuitive to increase the production of a compound that signals pain, but the ingenious action of capsaicin not only increases the release of substance P, it also blocks its reuptake by the nerve. After applying capsaicin to the affected area a

few times, the levels of substance P in the nerve endings of surrounding tissues have been spent, so there is nothing left to send the pain signal to the brain. Isn't Mother Nature amazing? Painkilling aside, topical application of chilli can have an immense stimulatory effect on circulation to that area. These two actions make it a perfect remedy for the stiffness caused by arthritis.

Chilli is also gaining a reputation as a potential weight loss tool. While I don't like 'magic' claims being made for individual ingredients, it is useful to be aware of such things. Again it is the spicy compound capsaicin that is reputed to deliver these effects. One study carried out in Taiwan suggests that capsaicin may be able to destroy cells called preadipocytes. These are juvenile cells that eventually turn into fat cells. Other small-scale studies have revealed that taking an extract of capsaicin increases the overall metabolic rate in test subjects, with some significant weight loss observed.

★ BEST WAY TO USE

Chilli does need to be used with caution, as it is so spicy. It can be used in cooking to generate the internal stimulating effects described above. It can also be puréed and applied directly to the skin for pain relief. For best results, cover this purée with a plaster or bandage.

CINNAMON

I adore the taste of this spice and it is a regular feature in a lot of my cooking. I find it has a comforting and nurturing quality. It has been used as a medicine in both Eastern and Western cultures for hundreds of years and has diverse applications.

The first application is gentle stimulation of the circulatory system. The essential oils contained in cinnamon are probably responsible for this effect. The likelihood is that these compounds relax the musculature of the vessel walls, leading to an overall widening of the vessel. This is a useful remedy for cold hands and feet. I also find that cinnamon is particularly useful for painful menstrual cramps, when improved blood flow in the pelvic region can improve the symptoms.

Cinnamon is a powerful antifungal agent, especially for fungal infections of the digestive tract, such as candidiasis. *Candida albicans* infection is drastically on the rise in modern society. With our increased intake of convenience foods, high sugar snacks, alcohol and yeasty breads, yeast infections of the gut are becoming more widespread and have been linked with food allergies, recurrent headaches, skin rashes and fatigue, to name but a few ailments. The number one key to tackling this type of infection is adopting a better diet and lifestyle, but there are herbs and remedies that can help. The powerful essential oils in cinnamon contain active compounds called cinnamaldehyde, cinnamyl acetate and cinnamyl alcohol that give it potent anti-fungal properties. These oils are believed to kill fungi such as yeasts and *Candida* on contact, so they slough off from the gut wall ready for expulsion via the bowel.

Cinnamon is gaining a considerable reputation as a blood sugar balancing agent that has proved to be useful in the management of type 2 diabetes. Type 2 diabetes is very different from the diabetes that individuals are born with or develop early on in life, which requires a lifetime of self-administered insulin injections. Type 2 diabetes is a disease of modern living. It is essentially a state in which the cells of the body have started to ignore the signal of insulin. Insulin is released when our blood sugar rises beyond a certain level. Its job is to tell the cells of the body that they need to pull this sugar in, and convert it into a usable energy source. This message is received via receptors that line the outside of cells in body tissues. Once the cells receive the signal, they take action.

When someone develops type 2 diabetes it is safe to assume that their blood sugar has been very high for a long time. By very high, I mean the type of sugar rush that comes from eating sugary snacks, refined white carbohydrates and drinking excessive alcohol. In the initial stages, cell receptors listen to the constant signalling from insulin that arises from such consumption. However, after a while the cell receptors start to suspect that something is awry. They wonder why there is so much insulin in circulation,

and think that maybe the insulin has gone a little crazy and doesn't know what it is doing. Therefore they begin to ignore its message. As a result of this, the levels of blood sugar start to rise as less and less of it is pulled into the cells. It is at this stage that type 2 diabetes is diagnosed. Cinnamon seems to directly influence structures on the outer surfaces of cells known as glucose transporters. These are used by cells to grab glucose from the blood and fluids that bathe the tissues, and pull it into the cells for conversion into energy. Studies suggest that cinnamon can increase the number produced and how effectively they take glucose from the circulation into the cell.

★ **BEST WAY TO USE**

To tap into its blood sugar management properties, cinnamon needs to be used quite liberally in cooking, and in smoothies and so on. Just a teaspoon or a shake of the powder is insufficient. Cinnamon can also be consumed as a tea made from the dried bark. Prepared in this way it acts as a gentle warming circulatory stimulant.

GARLIC

Garlic is one of the most powerful medicines on the planet, and its amazing properties could fill an entire book. It is a remedy that has benefits for virtually every system in the body. It is the pungent and powerful odour of garlic that is responsible for a large number of its medicinal properties. These compounds, also known as volatile factors, include the sulphur-based chemicals allicin, diallyl disulphide and diallyl trisulphide. Many of these chemicals become more active when garlic is crushed or chopped, as this starts an enzymatic process that releases more and more of them. These pungent-smelling chemicals act as effective antibacterial and antiviral agents. They are not broken down by the body and are excreted via, you guessed it, the breath (hence garlic's antisocial properties). These powerful chemicals destroy bacteria and viruses as they rush through the airways on exhalation. The compounds are also extremely active in the digestive tract and have a strong localised effect on any nasty invader in the gut, such as the yeast infection *Candida albicans*. The oils are powerful enough to kill this yeast on contact, and aid its removal from the body.

One of the properties of garlic that has been widely covered by the world's press for the last ten to fifteen years is the protective effect it has on the cardiovascular system. There are hundreds of studies that have shown that garlic offers some protection against the formation of plaques within artery walls. It is also well established that regular garlic consumption can help to lower the production of LDL (bad) cholesterol and increase the production of HDL (good) cholesterol. It is not 100 per cent clear how, but it may be due to interactions with the liver – the cholesterol-manufacturing plant. There are also some reported effects which reduce high blood pressure. It is believed that garlic is a very effective vasodilator, meaning that it can cause blood vessels to relax, which helps to lower overall pressure inside the vessels.

The sulphurous compounds in garlic also interact with enzymes that cause inflammation, giving it notable anti-inflammatory properties when consumed regularly. There is also some evidence to suggest that regular garlic consumption may offer protection against colon cancer, by preventing cells of the colon from damage (antimutagenic), and stopping cancerous cells from growing.

★ BEST WAY TO USE

Garlic is nearly always best used raw when you can stand it. Raw in salad dressings, sprinkled over roasted vegetables, added to various dishes at the last minute. Consuming it raw keeps the active chemicals intact. Whole slices of garlic can also be placed over fungal nail infections and secured with a plaster.

GINGER

This beautiful spice has been used in virtually every traditional healing system in the world, spanning millennia. It has been consumed in the traditional diets of almost every Asian country, and has become a very common ingredient in contemporary Western cookery too.

Ginger has traditionally been used for the treatment of stomach upsets such as nausea, morning sickness and travel sickness. It is also a great carminative agent, meaning that it can disperse wind and relieve intestinal bloating. Ginger is a wonderful circulatory stimulant as it relaxes the walls of the blood vessels, thus increasing blood flow. In this context it is a great remedy for cold extremities and conditions such as Reynaud's disease, in which circulation is greatly affected.

There is another exciting action that ginger offers, which is the one that I call on it most often for. It is a powerful anti-inflammatory and pain-relieving agent. A group of chemicals in ginger called gingerols is known to be anti-inflammatory. This is because they interfere with an enzyme called cyclo-oxygenase (COX) that is involved in switching on inflamma-tion and instigating pain. By blocking these enzymes, gingerols are able to prevent inflammation from occurring in the first place. Gingerols are also potent antioxi-dants, which can help reduce inflammation, because some inflammatory processes involve the release of free radicals. Free radicals are highly reactive biochemicals that cause all manner of damage and chaos in the body. Antioxidants are nutrients and plant chemicals that can deactivate the free radicals and protect body tissues from their destructive actions.

★ **BEST WAY TO USE**

As a juice, or added liberally to cooked dishes.

HORSERADISH

This staple of the British Sunday roast is a close relative of the cabbage. It has a long history of use in European herbal medicine. The leaves used to be a traditional salad vegetable, but it is the root that has given horseradish its reputation.

Horseradish contains a cocktail of volatile chemicals, including compounds such as myrosinase, that react together to give it a mustard-like flavour. It is this cocktail of chemicals that give rise to its most famous use – as a remedy for sinusitis. The mustard-like chemistry can rapidly thin mucus and reduce inflammation while stimulating circulation.

Horseradish has also been traditionally used as a cholagogue, which means that it helps to increase the flow of bile from the gall bladder. This offers a number of benefits. First, it means that the liver is able to remove broken down toxins faster. The liver uses bile to transport any toxins that aren't water-soluble and can't be flushed out via the kidneys. The bile carries these toxins into the intestine for removal via the bowel. Second, horseradish was also traditionally used as a potent diuretic, meaning that it helped to increase urinary flow. It was mixed with cider vinegar and honey, and taken in drop dosages throughout the day.

★ BEST WAY TO USE

Ideally, use the grated fresh root. However, this is extremely strong, so may not suit everyone. Also, it may not be easy to find. If fresh horseradish isn't available, a high-quality horseradish sauce will also provide equally impressive results.

MARJORAM (OREGANO)

Marjoram is a type of oregano. It is a staple herb in both Greek and Italian cooking. It has also been used medicinally for centuries.

It contains two strong aromatic oils – thymol and carvacol, which are believed to be responsible for the antimicrobial and natural antibiotic activity of marjoram. It has been traditionally used for food poisoning, amoebic dysentery and other digestive upsets.

Marjoram is also an effective carminative, meaning it helps to break down gas within the digestive tract, to reduce bloating and flatulence.

★ BEST WAY TO USE

Freshness is key. I find it heavenly added to dishes such as roasted vegetables and ratatouille. For relief of gas and bloating, I'd advise making a strong tea from the fresh leaves, and sipping slowly.

MINT

Mint has to be one of the most widely known and used herbs. It has a history of culinary and medicinal use in every culture, throughout all recorded periods of history and is a common feature in many gardens, parks and wild open spaces. It is native to the Mediterranean, and has played a part in traditions stemming from ancient Greece and ancient Rome. The Romans gave us the ever popular mint sauce found on many a Sunday dinner table.

Mint is a wonderful remedy for any kind of digestive discomfort. It is high in the essential oils carvacol, thymol and menthol (the oil responsible for the unmistakable smell). These powerful oils are highly effective carminatives, helping to break down and remove gas and wind from the digestive tract. The essential oils in mint are also very effective antispasmodics. This means they help to relax the muscles that line the walls of the digestive tract. This is useful for conditions such as irritable bowel syndrome and nervous diarrhoea.

Mint has also been traditionally used in cough and cold formulae. This is because the menthol content of mint has a reputation for 'tightening' up the mucus membranes, helping to dry up excessive mucous during a cold. Menthol is thought to be a diaphoretic, meaning that it encourages fever, thus helping to speed up infection recovery.

★ BEST WAY TO USE

Fresh is generally best. I'd advise growing your own, as it's an easy plant to look after in a pot on the windowsill, and then it is always on hand when you need it. For digestive problems, a tea made by infusing the fresh leaves in boiled water for 15–20 minutes is delicious and effective. It can also be eaten whole in any dish you fancy.

MUSTARD SEED

Mustard is a member of the cruciferous family of vegetables, that also includes broccoli, Brussels sprouts and cabbage. There are several different types, but the most commonly used is white mustard – the type that makes the yellow English mustard condiment that so many of us love. The ancient Romans are believed to have been the first to experiment with various ways of preparing mustard seeds. The best documented is the mixing of crushed mustard seeds with unfermented grape juice. This combination made a preparation that was nicknamed 'burning must', or in the language of that period 'mustum ardens'. Hence the word 'mustard' was born.

Mustard has been used medicinally since that period. The seeds are commonly used as a circulatory stimulant. The powerful essential oils that give mustard the distinctive fiery flavour can, like chilli peppers, cause a sudden and notable relaxation of the muscles within the blood vessel walls. Mustard has also been traditionally used as a poultice, applied directly to the chest to help relieve a chesty cough.

★ **BEST WAY TO USE**

Use the seeds in curries, or a good quality fresh mustard for a warming winter supplement or to loosen mucus.

PARSLEY

Parsley has become a bit of a cliché in the culinary world. For years, it was the herb used to decorate and garnish dishes, sprinkled haphazardly around the plate. It is also a classic ingredient in sauces for fish.

Parsley is a very powerful diuretic. It contains a strong essential oil (responsible for its fragrance and flavour) that acts as a very mild irritant to the filtration system in the kidney – the nephron. This irritation is harmless, yet enough to cause the kidney to increase the volume of urine that passes through at any one time. This makes parsley a great food to consider in cases of water retention. It should be avoided completely, however, if you have, or have recently had, a kidney infection or have any history of kidney disease.

★ **BEST WAY TO USE**

Use fresh in a salad or as a fragrant, earthy tea.

PEPPER

It's a fair assumption that pepper is on almost every table or in every kitchen in Europe and the US. It has become a universal seasoning. This everyday addition to food gives us an indication as to the way in which pepper was traditionally used as a medicine.

Pepper has long had a reputation for being a digestive aid. It is said to increase the force and regularity of peristaltic contractions (the rhythmic contractions that move gut contents along), and stimulate appetite. In Ayurveda, the traditional medical system of India, pepper is one of the favourite spices used to invigorate digestion, stimulate appetite and treat nausea. Pepper has such a powerful stimulatory – almost irritant – effect upon the digestive tract that some patients awaiting abdominal surgery are advised not to consume it.

Pepper is also a diaphoretic, so is useful for encouraging a fever, which can help to reduce recovery time when fighting an infection.

★ BEST WAY TO USE

Pepper can be incorporated into a herbal tea blend (pure pepper tea is not advisable) or added directly to food. For weak digestion and poor appetite, a teaspoonful of ground black pepper can be taken, washed down with a small glass of water.

ROSEMARY

Rosemary is one of the most commonly sold, grown and used herbs in the UK. It is a vigorous plant which can take over a herb garden very easily if not kept in check. It is a native of the Mediterranean and has been a part of Greek culture for centuries.

In Greece, it was traditionally used to enhance and to stimulate memory. This use still holds strong today, and rosemary is commonly used in Western medical herbalism for forgetfulness and a fuzzy head. This property comes from its essential oils. These powerful oils, like those in many culinary herbs, cause a widening of the blood vessels. This enhancement of circulation improves blood flow to the brain, and is believed to be the reason rosemary delivers such improvements to memory. Rosemary is also commonly used to enhance circulation. Conditions such as cold fingers and toes benefit greatly from the regular consumption of rosemary.

Rosemary has become a popular anti-inflammatory herb of late. It contains a powerful antioxidant compound called rosmaric acid. Some encouraging recent trials have suggested that rosmaric acid combats inflammation by causing a localised reduction in some of the chemicals that encourage inflammation.

Rosemary is also antispasmodic (helps to calm digestive cramps) and a diuretic.

As a tea, or added fresh (don't overcook or process) to meals such as roasted vegetables, breads, potato dishes and so on.

SAGE

Sage is another of our most widely grown and widely used herbs. A staple of British cuisine, sage appears on many a Sunday dinner plate. Who can resist some sage and onion stuffing?

Sage is viewed as a sacred plant in many cultures. It has been used in blessing ceremonies by Catholic priests, Native Americans and some South American cultures. It is also often used for 'smudging'. This is the burning of sage tied in a bundle to 'clear the energy' of a room or space.

Sage has gained the reputation of being an effective remedy for hot flushes associated with the menopause. It is often recommended as a tea while experiencing a hot flush. It is not entirely clear how sage affects hot flushes, but its anecdotal track record is impressive. It is also believed to be antihidrotic, meaning it reduces perspiration. In addition, it is believed to reduce lactation, so pregnant or breastfeeding women should avoid consuming sage in large quantities.

Sage is a renowned antibiotic agent.

It contains powerful fragrant essential oils that seem to be very good at killing harmful oral bacteria. This is why sage has been a popular ingredient in herbal mouthwashes and breath fresheners. Many people believe that this was one of the major reasons that sage was originally included in many meat-based recipes – to help destroy harmful bacteria that may be in the food. It was also used as a compress, applied directly to wounds, to minimise the risk of infection. Sage is also believed to be a stimulant, general tonic and memory aid.

★ BEST WAY TO USE

As with many herbs and spices, fresh is always best. Take as a strong tea for hot flushes, or incorporate into salads or cooked dishes for its general tonic properties.

THYME

Another of the classics, thyme is one of the true garden heroes. It is another Mediterranean staple that has become commonplace in British cuisine, and is frequently used in casseroles, breads, on pizzas and in many meat-based dishes.

Thyme is also a staple ingredient in any herbalist's medicine cabinet. It is very high in three exceptionally powerful essential oils – borneol, geraniol and thymol. These potent oils give thyme its renowned antibacterial properties.

The most interesting property of thyme is the evidence emerging that it may be highly beneficial to the health of the brain. Early studies suggest that something in thyme's chemistry enables it to increase the levels of a certain fat, called DHA, into cell membranes. DHA is created in our bodies from dietary omega 3, from sources such as nuts, seeds and avocados. It is used to maintain the structure of cells and tissues, and is most widely found in nerve cells. In the brain and nervous system, the cells have a unique and specialised structure. They have large, elongated, fatty capsules along their entire length. These capsules do not touch, however. There is a tiny gap between the point where one capsule ends and the next starts. As you may know, every cell in the brain and nervous system communicates with the next via electrical signals. To make these signals travel at high speed, the cell allows the electrical signal to jump along the cell surface,

using these little unexposed areas between capsules. The fatty substance DHA is vital for keeping the structure and function of this system in check. So by ensuring that we have healthy levels of DHA in the cells, we can help these cells to work to their optimal potential, and it is here that the consumption of thyme looks most promising.

★ BEST WAY TO USE

Thyme is traditionally used as a gargle, and seems to be particularly effective in treating strep throat infections and tonsillitis. When used topically, thyme is also a potent antifungal.

TURMERIC

Turmeric, the staple ingredient of Indian curries, belongs to the same family as ginger, and shares some of its properties. It is a knobbly brown root with vivid orange flesh and a zingy invigorating aroma. Turmeric has been used in traditional Indian Ayurvedic herbal practices for centuries, and has even made its way into cosmetic products.

Like ginger, turmeric is a powerful anti-inflammatory agent. The chemicals that give turmeric its distinctive vibrant yellow/orange colour are key to its powerful inflammation-busting activity. These are a chemical group known as curcuminoids. In clinical trials the anti-inflammatory activity of these compounds has been shown to be comparable with such powerful drugs as hydrocortisone, phenylbutazone, indomethacin and neurophen. These amazing compounds reduce inflammation by blocking the activity of a group of chemical messengers called prostaglandins. You may recall from previous sections of this book that prostaglandins are a group of chemical compounds made in the body from dietary fats. Part of their physiological role is to regulate the inflammatory response. This involves a series of chemical reactions that finally lead to a localised inflammatory response. Curcuminoids from turmeric block the normal progress of these chemical reactions and prevent them from reaching their goal.

Turmeric is also a great spice for the health of the heart and cardiovascular system. It is what herbalists refer to as 'anti-platelet'. Platelets are small, disc-like cells within the blood that are involved in the formation of blood clots, and are the agents at play when a scab forms. Clotting is a vital process that protects us from bleeding to death as a result of the smallest cut, and allows us to heal internal injuries rapidly. However, it is problematic when our blood clots excessively, as this, along with other active risk factors, puts us at greater risk of heart attack and stroke. Turmeric helps to reduce the platelets' clotting capacity – not to the extent that it becomes dangerous, but enough to offer a bit of extra protection against heart attacks.

Turmeric is also believed to be hepato-protective. This means that it may help to protect the liver from damage. The bright orange pigments, the curcuminoids, are also very powerful antioxidants. This is the most likely reason why turmeric offers this protection to the liver.

★ **BEST WAY TO USE**

In curries or tea; ideally in fresh form if you can get it, or powdered is fine.

VEGETABLES

I think it is fair to say that we have more of a love/hate relationship with vegetables than with any other food. Once the staple of our diet, vegetables are now being consumed on an alarmingly reduced scale. I have first-hand experience of working with people under the age of twenty, who had no idea what simple vegetables such as beetroot, sweet potatoes and courgettes were. This seems to be representative of modern dietary trends – trends that can, and most likely will, deliver severe health consequences for future generations.

The term vegetable isn't a scientific or botanical term. It generally describes an edible plant, or a plant with edible portions, that doesn't fall into the botanical class of fruit or seed. However, that is as far as the distinctions go, so the term can often be rather arbitrary. Some may consider mushrooms and avocados vegetables, whereas others may not.

Vegetables are the most suitable foods for human consumption, above all other food categories, and offer some of the most profound and complex medicinal effects found in the plant kingdom. Some have powerful colour pigments that can offer protection against chemical damage, or even speed up or slow down certain functions. Some deliver their medicinal activity via complex flavours, while others offer us therapeutic benefit through the action of the chemicals they produce naturally during normal growth.

ASPARAGUS

I love asparagus, especially lightly steamed with a little melted butter and black pepper. Heaven! It is also a nutrient-dense and medicinal vegetable. First, it has proved to be a very effective diuretic agent, thanks to a nitrogenous compound called asparagine. This is why asparagus has been used in the past as a tonic for kidney health and fluid retention. If kidney output is stimulated, then a more rapid removal of excessive fluids in the body will ensue. This stimulation will give the kidneys a flush too, helping to remove metabolic waste and debris.

Asparagus is also showing potential as an anti-inflammatory food. It contains a powerful phytochemical called racemofuran, which is believed to work similarly to a group of anti-inflammatory drugs called COX-2 inhibitors. This means it can partially block the chemical chain reactions that arise when an inflammatory response is activated.

Some members of the asparagus family have been used for centuries in traditional Indian Ayurvedic medicine to increase fertility and regulate the menstrual cycle, and many believe culinary asparagus has the same properties. There is little data available at present that supports this, however.

★ BEST WAY TO USE

Steam or sauté. Do *not* boil!

AUBERGINE

I love these Mediterranean delights. Aubergines are like big sponges that will suck up almost any flavour that is added to them.

Aubergine has often been seen as having little in the way of nutrition or major health benefit, apart from being a good source of dietary fibre. However, in recent years, a compound called nasunin was discovered in the skin. Nasunin has been shown to protect the fatty membranes of cells within the nervous system and brain from chemical damage. Scientists now believe that long-term consumption may offer some protection against degenerative mental disorders such as dementia.

★ BEST WAY TO USE

Lightly cooked, roasted and puréed to make baba ganoush.

BEETROOT

Beetroot has to be one of my favourite vegetables. There is nothing quite like big chunks of slow-roasted beetroot with horseradish sauce as an accompaniment to Sunday lunch. It is from the same family as spinach and chard, and comes in many different varieties, with colours ranging from white through to vivid golden yellow. Here, however, we will focus on the common, deep purple variety.

The deep purple pigment that gives beetroot its characteristic colour, and stains almost anything it touches, is part of the key to beetroot's medicinal properties. This vivid pigment is a compound called betacyanin. Betacyanin has been shown to increase certain chemical functions in the liver that form part of what is known as phase 2 detoxification. It essentially speeds up certain chemical reactions that are involved in the smooth running of this process. Phase 2 detoxification is one of the series of processes that the liver uses to turn harmful toxins, such as alcohol and metabolic wastes, into harmless substances that can easily be removed from the body. This makes beetroot a useful food for detoxification and liver-cleansing.

Beetroot is also known to have a beneficial effect upon blood pressure. It contains chemicals called nitrates. When we consume nitrates, they are converted by the body into a compound called nitric oxide. Nitric oxide is a powerful vasodilator (widens blood vessels). It does this by forcing a sudden relaxation of the muscular walls that line the blood vessels. When these muscles relax, the internal size of the vessel increases, so the pressure within the vessel naturally decreases.

Beetroot is also believed to be a powerful anti-cancer food. This is because it increases the production of one of the body's own anti-cancer chemicals, produced to protect cells from damage. This protective chemical is a compound called glutathione S-transferase.

★ **BEST WAY TO USE**

Juiced, grated raw or roasted in big chunks.

BROCCOLI

Broccoli, like cabbage and cauliflower, is a member of the cruciferous vegetable family. Unlike most of the foods in this book, broccoli doesn't have a fast-acting medicinal effect. It does, however, have some very powerful disease-preventing properties that warrant its inclusion.

Broccoli is probably the most highly regarded food for cancer prevention. This is due to the high levels of three powerful cancer-fighting phytochemical groups – isothiocyanates, indoles and dithiolethiones. These almost unpronounceable chemicals protect the body from cancer by regulating the way in which cells respond to environmental elements that can potentially trigger cancerous changes within the DNA of the cell. They do this by increasing the cell's natural defence mechanisms against damage, making it more resistant.

★ BEST WAY TO USE

As fresh as possible. Steamed, stir-fried or raw.

CABBAGE

Without doubt, cabbage is our most affordable vegetable, and one of the most powerful foods you can include in your weekly diet. Better still, cabbages are easy to grow, so you can even raise your own supply of fresh, homegrown super greens.

Cabbages contain a cocktail of phytochemicals that can have a huge impact upon the normal detoxification of the cells in all our tissues. They do this by encouraging the DNA of each cell to produce more enzymes that enable and facilitate the detoxification and breakdown of harmful toxic material.

Cabbages also contain phytochemicals indole-3-carbinol and isothiocyanates, which have potent anti-cancer properties.

There is a link between cabbage consumption and lowered risk of heart disease. This is because cabbage can lower a compound called homocysteine. Although it is not clear whether homocysteine itself plays a role in the development of heart disease, or whether its presence is an indicator of other risks, lowering elevated levels definitely does reduce heart attack risk.

★ BEST WAY TO USE

Steamed, sautéed or raw. Boiled cabbage is of no use to man or beast. Boiling this precious vegetable will render it devoid of the good stuff.

CARROTS

Although quite often found boiled to the point of semi-existence, carrots can be incredibly powerful both nutritionally and medicinally.

The bright orange colour of carrots is due to the massive concentration of the plant source of vitamin A, called beta-carotene. This chemical is a colour pigment from the carotenoid group, responsible for colours ranging from pale yellow to dark red in the plant kingdom. Beta-carotene is beneficial for the heart and cardiovascular system, by helping to protect the structural integrity of the inner lining of the blood vessels, thus helping to reduce the rupture and injury that can lead to the formation of clots.

Beta-carotene is also famous for improving eye health. First, it improves night vision, hence the old wives' tale that carrots help you see in the dark. Second, it is known to protect an area of the eye known as the macula densa; the area that can suffer macular degeneration. This age-associated damage to the eye is caused by the activity of free radicals. Beta-carotene has an affinity with this tissue, and is extremely good at disarming this type of free radical.

★ BEST WAY TO USE

Raw, grated or as a crudité with a dip such as hummus. This combination is especially good, as the fats in the hummus will help the beta-carotene to be absorbed faster.

CELERY

This stringy salad staple is one of those foods that people either love or hate, and sometimes getting it down many of my clients can be a real challenge. But this vegetable that we think is dull and useless is, in fact, a very powerful medicinal food.

Celery contains a compound called 3-n-butylphthalide, which is a powerful pain-killer. Useful for treating arthritis, sprains and chronic pain, its effect isn't as long-lasting as a prescription painkiller, but it is a beautiful example of a simple food that can be incorporated into your diet regularly to assist in overall healing and comfort.

Celery also contains a fragrant group of chemicals called coumarins. These are part of the chemistry that give celery its distinct smell. Coumarins help to stimulate the lymphatic system, which is the main system that drains and clears waste and gunk that is released from the tissues. Coumarins help to increase uptake of excessive fluids by the lymphatic system, and they also have a mild diuretic property, which further supports their ability to remove excess fluid from the body. This makes celery an ideal food for cycle-related fluid retention and arthritis (it removes fluid build-up from joints) and it can even help with lowering blood pressure.

★ BEST WAY TO USE

Eaten raw or juiced.

FENNEL

Fennel is a vegetable that some people see in the supermarket, pick up with a semi-bewildered expression and then put back and move on. It is overlooked. This is unfortunate, because fennel has some wonderful health-giving properties, it is such an easy vegetable to prepare and it has a glorious flavour.

Fennel contains a beautifully fragrant essential oil called anethol. Anethol has been shown to be a very powerful anti-inflammatory. It reduces the number of certain chemical signals released by some white blood cells that encourage localised inflammation. Anethol is also the main chemical responsible for fennel's famous antispasmodic effect. This means it helps to reduce and regulate normal contractions of the gut wall. This makes fennel useful in cases of painful abdominal cramps and IBS. The essential oils in fennel are also carminative, meaning they help to reduce and disperse gas from the digestive tract.

Fennel is also relatively high in phytoestrogens. These are plant chemicals similar in chemical structure to the female hormone oestrogen and are known to be of use in any condition where a change in oestrogen levels is causing symptoms, such as during menopause and to address premenstrual issues. In cases where oestrogen levels are very low, it is believed that phytoestrogens are able to make the body think that there is more oestrogen available than there really is. In cases where oestrogen is too high, it is believed that phytooestrogens can compete against natural oestrogen for binding sites on the outer surfaces of cells, thus reducing oestrogen's impact. If levels of the body's own oestrogen are high, then there is possibility of too much delivering its specific responses. If phytoestrogens are competing with the body's own estrogen for receptor binding sites, and is not biologically active, there will be less sites for the body's own oestrogen to bind to and cause changes in cell and tissues.

★ **BEST WAY TO USE**

Sliced raw or lightly roasted. The fine top foliage can be chopped and eaten raw.

GLOBE ARTICHOKE

You might have seen the globe artichoke in the supermarket, and thought, 'hmm – looks nice, but I have no idea what to do with it'! An unopened flower, the outer leaves are inedible, but the central flesh (the heart) is heavenly to eat.

Globe artichokes contain a group of chemicals called caffeoylquinic acids. These compounds are the reason the artichoke has traditionally been used to treat liver disorders, as it increases the flow of bile from the liver. The liver uses bile to transport toxins it has broken down that need to be removed from the body. Bile also aids the digestion and absorption of fat, so eating artichoke with a fatty meal is beneficial.

Artichoke may be able to lower cholesterol by affecting how it is broken down in the liver. This could be due to artichoke's ability to speed up the exit of fatty material (used to make cholesterol) out of the liver.

Artichoke is also believed to be an ideal diabetic food because it is high in a special kind of sugar known as inulin. Inulin is believed to play a beneficial role in blood sugar management, helping other sugars consumed alongside it to be released into the bloodstream at a far slower pace.

★ BEST WAY TO USE

Lightly roasted or baked. As fresh as possible.

KALE

Kale has to be one of my favourite foods. It is wholesome and filling and leaves me feeling wonderful after I have eaten it.

Kale is an especially useful food for those with high cholesterol, because it contains a chemical called indole-3-carbinol. This miraculous compound reduces the production of a cholesterol-carrying molecule called apolipoprotein B-100. This is one of the main transporter chemicals involved in carrying cholesterol away from the liver to the other tissues in the body, which may lead to a harmful build-up. Indole-3-carbinol reduces this cholesterol by around 56 per cent. This clever compound also seems to have an impact on the extent to which the liver manufactures blood lipids (fats), which can lead to elevated cholesterol.

Kale, like all the brassicas, contains a very high level of sulphur-based compounds, including glucosinolates, which help to increase cells' ability to process and break down potentially cancerous chemicals. There is a long-accepted link between the consumption of cruciferous vegetables and a reduced risk of developing cancers. This is most likely the reason why.

★ BEST WAY TO USE

Delicious eaten raw. Drizzle with olive oil and a pinch of salt, and massage to wilt the leaves. If you cook it, steam it lightly or stir-fry quickly.

LEEKS

I never liked leeks particularly, but now I just can't get enough of them. Every Sunday, I have leeks with butter and black pepper as an accompaniment to Sunday lunch.

Leeks, like all the alliums, are very high in sulphur-based compounds such as allicin that can help to reduce clotting in the blood, and can have a notable antiviral effect. These compounds also play a role in naturally lowering cholesterol and protect against certain cancers.

Another interesting cancer-fighting phytochemical is found in leeks – a compound called kaempferol. A well-known Nurses' Health Study that ran between 1984 and 2002 revealed that women with the highest intake of kaempferol had a 40 per cent reduction in their risk of developing ovarian cancer. While this observational study hasn't been backed up by further clinical data, it certainly gives some interesting information about the potential properties of this often underrated allium.

★ BEST WAY TO USE

Any way really. I have a preference for sautéing them in olive oil and butter, with a good pinch of sea salt and black pepper. Also great in soups.

ONIONS

One of the kings of the vegetable kingdom without a shadow of doubt. I use them in nearly every savoury dish I make. I especially love red onions. The gorgeous red/purple pigment delivers higher levels of antioxidants than their white counterparts.

Onions are a very rich source of an antioxidant compound called quercetin, which is an effective natural antihistamine. Histamine is a chemical released locally by white blood cells when they are exposed to certain stimuli that cause allergic symptoms. This localised histamine release causes symptoms such as the itching, sneezing, inflammation and so on that we associate with allergy. Quercetin appears to be very effective at reducing the ability of these cells to release their histamine when stimulated.

Onions are also believed to be potent anti-inflammatories – especially for the respiratory tract. They contain compounds that have been shown to inhibit the effect of specific communication chemicals that increase the production of pro-inflammatory prostaglandins (see the Joints chapter, pages 127–151). These body chemicals, called lipoxygenase and cyclo-oxygenase, are substances that cause a drastic shift in the production of these problematic inflammatory stimulants, so any natural substances that reduce this can reduce the severity and duration of inflammatory episodes. Onions aren't as powerful as a high-strength drug, but like foods such as ginger and turmeric, they are ideal for helping to reduce inflammation.

Red onions in particular are a favourite daily staple to help support cardiovascular health. This is due to the chemistry of the purple colour pigment. The key here is a group of compounds called flavonoids. These have been extensively researched in the UK, and have been found to stimulate the release of nitric oxide from the endothelium (the inner skin that lines blood vessels). Nitric oxide then relaxes the muscles that make up the vessel walls. This causes the vessel to dilate, lowering the pressure within. Regular consumption of flavonoid-rich foods can help to reduce blood pressure.

Onions are also a wonderful food for overall digestive health. They contain a fabulous compound called inulin that works as a prebiotic agent. This means that it encourages the growth of good bacteria in the gut, by providing them with a food source. This helps to increase the number of the good, and decrease the number of the bad, fine-tuning digestive health when consumed regularly.

★ **BEST WAY TO USE**

Raw or lightly sautéed.

PEPPERS

These crunchy salad vegetables pack a powerful punch, both medicinally and nutritionally. From the nutritional perspective, they are very high in vitamin C, some of the B vitamins and also vitamin A.

Peppers, especially red ones, are very dense in compounds called carotenoids. These are colour pigments in plants that can range from yellows to oranges to reds. These powerful pigments have a strong antioxidant activity and have been linked with increased protection against cancers. They are also believed to play a role in slowing down age-related damage to the eyes, and offer protection against cataracts.

★ **BEST WAY TO USE**

Raw or very lightly stir-fried or sautéed.

POTATOES

Once considered the dieter's enemy, these starchy staples are going through something of a renaissance. I have to admit, I didn't eat them often, but now Sundays and roast potatoes have a symbiotic relationship in my eyes! And now that new research has revealed some amazing chemical properties, I can eat them almost guilt free.

New research has identified a compound in potatoes called kukoamine. This rare compound is found in some Chinese herbs, and nobody expected it to turn up in the humble spud! Kukoamine has been shown to lower blood pressure. Research is still in the early stages and nobody is sure how kukoamine does this, or indeed how many potatoes need to be consumed to have a significant impact.

★ BEST WAY TO USE

Generally, steamed, boiled or baked. Keep consumption of roasted/fried potatoes to a minimum – roasties are best as a once a week treat.

SPINACH

Popeye's famous staple food, spinach is one of the most powerful foods on the planet. First, it is a nutrient-packed power-house. It contains more usable protein, gram for gram, than sirloin steak, more usable calcium than any dairy product and a whole host of B vitamins.

More exciting than this, though, is the huge array of cancer-fighting compounds found in spinach. It contains a group of 13 or 14 flavonoid chemicals. These compounds have proved so powerful that they have prompted myriad clinical trials with spinach extracts. These have shown a high level of protection against cancers of the stomach, prostate and ovaries. The picture is especially interesting in the case of prostate cancer. One of the chemical fractions of the chemical group mentioned above is a compound called neoxanthin. This amazing phytochemical has been shown to force cancerous prostate cells into a state known as 'apoptosis', which is the suicide state programmed into every cell in the body. When this function is stimulated, the cell dies in minutes. The fascinating story doesn't end there. When neoxanthin is digested and processed in the intestines, a certain pro-portion is converted into a substance called neochromes. This substance puts cancerous prostate cells into a state of stasis, which helps to slow down major progression of the disease. So what are you waiting for; get that spinach down you!

★ BEST WAY TO USE

Raw is absolutely the best way to consume spinach, and it is the base of virtually all my salads. You can also steam and sauté it. Boiled spinach, however, is about as much use as an ashtray on a motorbike, so forget that idea!

SWEET POTATOES

I love sweet potatoes. I love the colour, the texture and the delicious sweet flavour. Sweet potatoes are a very dense and rich source of the potent antioxidant beta-carotene. This is the compound responsible for sweet potatoes' characteristic bright orange colour. Beta-carotene is not only the plant form of vitamin A, it is also a powerful anti-inflammatory. Its antioxidant activity buffers some of the inflammatory activity delivered by white blood cells.

Beta-carotene is also great for skin health. This is because it is a fat-soluble antioxidant. It quickly leaves the bloodstream and migrates into fatty tissues where it can accumulate. After the brain, the most abundant fatty tissue in the body is the subcutaneous layer of the skin. Fat-soluble antioxidants such as carotenoids can accumulate here and offer localised protection to structures such as collagen and elastin.

Sweet potatoes also contain a unique protein. This is a storage protein that the plant uses as a food source while it is growing. This fantastic protein is what is known as an immunomodulator, meaning it can help to regulate certain responses within the immune system. Again, much of the research into this activity is in the early stages. What we do know, however, is that it interacts with elements of the immune system that instigate and worsen the inflammatory response.

I find sweet potatoes wonderful for digestive health. They contain a sugar called fructo-oligosaccharide (FOS). This sugar is a prebiotic, meaning that it can encourage the growth of good bacteria in the gut. When the population of good bacteria in our digestive system feeds on this sugar, they begin to reproduce, thus increasing the colony. That's not all. When the good bacteria feed upon FOS, they produce a chemical called butyric acid that can repair and strengthen the gut wall, helping to regenerate and rejuvenate the digestive tract.

Sweet potatoes are believed to be very good for diabetics. It appears that they can help to stabilise blood sugar levels and to improve cells' responsiveness to insulin. It isn't yet clear why this happens.

★ BEST WAY TO USE

I love them baked, in place of the traditional baked potato. They are also great in soups, curries and roasted with garlic.

RECIPES BY HEALTH BENEFITS

You will have noticed that many of the ingredients mentioned in this book occur in recipes in more than one section – their medicinal benefits stretching to more than one part of the body. Below you will find the recipes sorted accordingly, showing you which parts of the body the recipes can apply to.

RECIPE	PAGE	Skin Health	The Digestive System	The Heart and Circulatory System	The Immune System	The Joints	The Nervous System
Apple jacks	95			X			X
Brown rice bibimbap	164	X		X	X	X	X
Celery ginger juice shot	144	X		X	X	X	X
Chickpea, squash and rainbow chard curry	44	X	X	X	X	X	X
Chocolate orange truffle torte	96	X		X			X
Cinnamon flax granola	82	X		X	X		X
Classic carrot and ginger soup	35	X	X	X	X	X	
Coconut porridge with berry ginger compote	161	X		X	X	X	X
Coconut porridge with spiced roasted pear purée	84			X			X

Recipe	Page						
Dhal Soup	65	X	X	X	X	X	
Fig and chia bars	58	X	X	X	X		X
Goji berry and pumpkin seed energy bombs	115	X			X		X
Goji berry hummus	116	X	X	X	X	X	
Lavender and rose chocolate	168			X			X
Leek and sweet potato frittata	62	X	X			X	
Mackerel kedgeree	162	X	X	X	X	X	X
Miso ginger salmon and caraway purée	37	X		X	X	X	X
Miso mackerel with spicy kale	150	X	X	X	X	X	X
Mussels in tomato chilli sauce	118	X	X	X	X	X	
Pan-fried mackerel with slow-cooked barley and red cabbage slaw	90	X	X	X	X	X	X
Prawn, shiitake and spring onion speedy noodles	120	X	X	X	X	X	X
Prawns and greens in satay sauce	42	X	X	X	X	X	X
Red ratatouille and bulgar wheat stack	94	X	X	X	X	X	X
Roasted beetroot, caramelised red onion, puy lentil and goat's cheese warm salad	88	X	X	X			
Roasted Jerusalem artichoke, red onion and feta salad	60	X	X	X	X	X	X
Roasted red onion, squash and feta salad	86	X	X	X			X

Roasted red pepper and sweet potato soup	36	X	X	X	X	X	
Roasted sweet potato, smoked salmon, goat's cheese and walnut salad	38	X	X	X		X	X
Seafood linguine	122	X	X	X	X	X	X
Sesame soy salmon with spiced butternut purée and pineapple salsa	148	X	X	X	X	X	X
Shiitake sunflower spread	85	X	X	X	X	X	X
Speedy salmon curry	145	X	X	X	X	X	X
Spiced fish soup with ginger and turmeric	146	X	X	X	X	X	X
Spicy chickpeas	89	X	X	X	X	X	
Spinach-stuffed chicken with red pepper pesto, white beans and citrus watercress	92	X	X	X	X	X	X
Squash croquettes with minted avocado dipping sauce	40	X	X	X			
Surf and turf	166	X	X	X	X	X	X
Sweet potato and white bean stew	45	X	X	X	X	X	
Sweet potato gnocchi with baby spinach and red pepper sauce	46	X	X	X	X	X	X
Tummy tea	64	X	X				X
Turbo-charged chicken soup	117	X	X	X	X	X	
Wasabi salmon with gingered greens	163	X		X	X	X	X

GENERAL INDEX

acne 25–6, 28, 34

alcohol 71, 171, 201, 215

allergies 26, 182, 188, 200, 220

amaranth 187

anchovy 139

aniseed 196

antibiotic 181, 195, 204, 209

antibodies 102, 106, 138

antifungal agents 200

antioxidants 30, 33, 34, 46, 78, 80, 99, 125, 176, 177, 179, 180, 187, 188, 191, 203, 208, 211, 220, 221, 223

apples 75, 77, 175–6

arthritis 200, 217, *see also* rheumatoid and osteoarthritis

artichoke:

   globe 67, 218

   Jerusalem 56, 67

articular cartilage 128, 134, 135, 138

asparagus 214

asthma 26, 175, 176, 196

aubergine 214

avocado 33, 77, 210, 213

axons 154

Ayurvedic traditions 11, 195, 208, 211, 214

bacteria 21, 22, 26, 29, 52, 53, 54, 56, 57, 101, 102, 103, 104, 107, 108, 125, 179, 188, 202, 209, 210, 221, 223

banana 176

barley, pearl 80, 156

basil 197

bay leaves 56, 67

beetroot 17, 34, 77, 213, 215

beriberi 12

berries 72

beta-carotene 33, 34, 78, 181, 217, 223

betacyanin 17, 34, 215

blackberries 75, 158

blood 70–1, *see also* circulatory system

  cells:

    red 70

    white 24, 29, 30, 34, 54, 70, 102, 103, 109, 110, 111, 113, 114, 151, 179, 188, 191, 218, 220, 223

  clots 72, 73, 77, 79, 81, 180, 188, 211, 217, 220

  pressure/flow 71, 73, 77, 78, 158, 176, 177, 198, 202, 215, 217, 221, 222

  sugar levels 73, 171, 185, 201, 223

vessels 24, 25, 69, 71, 72, 77, 78, 80, 81, 104, 109, 158, 176, 187, 188, 196, 198, 202, 203, 208, 215, 217, 221

blueberry 158, 177, 179

Body Mass Index (BMI) 12, 16

bones 127–33

    cells in 128–9

    diseases of 127, 129–33

    health, foods for 139–40

    nutritional management of 132–3

    structure of 127–9

Brazil nuts 191

bread 51, 53, 125, 151, 200, 210

broccoli 109, 216

bronchitis 196

buckwheat 188

butternut squash 30, 33, 78

cabbage 207, 216

cacao 78, 158

calcium 78, 130, 131, 132–3, 139, 143, 192, 222

calories 12, 16, 185

cancer 176, 177, 181, 185, 192, 194, 202, 215, 216, 219, 220–222

carbohydrates 11, 12, 51, 52, 53, 54, 67, 105, 125, 151, 176, 185, 201

cardamom 198

cardiovascular disease 13

carminatives 67, 196, 203, 204, 205, 218

carotenoids 30, 31, 34, 221, 223

carrots 30, 33, 196, 217

cavolo nero 143, 158

celery 142, 196, 217

chard, rainbow 34

cheese, full fat 139

cherries 177

chickpea 33, 78

chilli 113, 198–200, 207

Chinese medicine 11, 195, 197

chocolate 72, 158–9, *see also* cacao

cholesterol 23, 72, 73, 75, 77, 78, 79, 80, 81, 94, 98, 132, 175, 179, 180, 187, 188, 194, 202, 219, *see also* circulatory system

cinnamon 200–1

circulatory system 69–99

    cardiovascular disease 13

    food for 176, 198, 203, 207, 208, 211, 217

    health of 69, 71–5

    RECIPES FOR 77–97

citrus fruit 31, 109, *see also* oranges

coconut 192

constipation 52

courgette 213

cranberry 179

dates 179

dermis 24

detoxification 34, 215, 216

diaphysis 127

diabetes 185, 187, 201, 219, 223

diarrhoea 187, 205

diet and health 11–13, 15–17

    nutritional supplements 15

digestion 56, 72

    ailments of 15

    food beneficial for 56–7, 198, 205, 221

    health, tips for 67

    RECIPES FOR 59–65

    system 51–67

        healthy transit in 52–3

dill 196

diuretics 204, 207, 208, 214, 217

E. coli 179

eczema 26, 27, 34

endosteum 128

essential fatty acids (EFAS) 109–10

Egyptian medicine 11

endothelium 71, 72–3, 75, 104

epidermis 23–4, 25

epiphysis 128

role of, the 133–5
   functional classification of 134
   structural classification of 134

kale 219
kiwi fruit 31, 109

Langerhan cells 22, 25
lavender 159
leek 67, 220
lemon 181
lentils, puy 80
lime 181
lipid, 80, 219, *see also* fats

mackerel 27, 74, 79, 137, 143, 155, 159
macrophages 25, 103, 104
magnesium 78, 133, 140, 143, 156, 158, 192
mango 30, 31, 181
margerine and fatty acid 74
marjoram 204
medullary cavity 128
melon 30
menopause 130, 209, 218
micronutrients 12
minerals 12, 99, 128, 133, 175, 191
mint 67, 197, 205
mushroom 108, 113, 179, 188
   shiitake, for fighting infection 29–30, 80, 108,
     111, 114, 179, 188
mustard seed 207
mussels 114
myelin sheath 154, 155, 156, 159

nervous system 153–71
   central nervous system (CNS) 153
   diet for 155
   key foods for 155–6
   medicinal benefits for 158–9

peripheral nervous system (PNS) 153
RECIPES FOR 161–8
neurons 154
neurotransmitterrs 154, 155, 156, 158, 159
neutrophils 103–4
nuts 79, 110, 155, 191–2, 210

oats 67, 72, 75, 78, 79, 80, 159, 188
oils, cooking and fatty acid 74
omegas, *see* fats
onions 33, 54, 56, 57, 67, 79, 220
   red 17, 75, 79–80
oranges 30, 80
oregano, *see* marjoram
osteoarthritis 135–6
   dealing with 136–7
osteoblasts 128
osteoclasts 128, 129, 130, 133
osteocytes 128–9
osteomalacia 129, 131, 132
osteoporosis 127, 129–31, 132

pain 13, 23, 27, 98, 131, 136, 138, 177, 196, 198,
     200, 203, 217, 218
painkillers 195, 198, 203, 217
papaya 182
parsley 207
pasta 53, 125, 151, 187, 188
pathogens 21, 22, 25, 29, 54, 70, 101, 102, 103,
     104, 105, 107, 109, 111, 113, 114
pears 80
pectin 75, 77, 175, 176
peppers 31, 34, 80, 207, 221
periostium 128, 134
peristalsis 53, 54, 56, 57, 67, 107, 196
phytochemicals 15–17
phytosterol 78, 80, 81
pineapple, as an anti-inflammatory 28, 138, 182
polysaccharides 30, 108, 111, 113, 114

potassium 176, 192

potato 222

prawn 34, 114

prostaglandins 13, 27–8, 34, 74, 79, 110, 113, 136, 138, 143, 151, 211, 220

proteins 11, 12, 24, 30, 52, 70, 71, 98, 102, 103, 104, 105, 135, 136, 140, 151, 181, 182, 187, 189, 223

psoriasis 26, 34

pulses 54, 67, 99

pumpkin seed, for fighting infection 29, 49, 109, 111, 114, 194

refined food 13, 53, 125, 151, 185, 201, see also sugar

rheumatoid arthritis 137–8
    anti-inflammatories for 138

rice 125
    brown 53, 156, 158, 185, 187
    white 53, 151, 185

rickets 12, 127, 129, 131, 132

rose 159

rosemary 208

sage 209

salmon 27, 34, 74, 75, 131, 137, 142, 155, 159

sardine 27, 131, 139

scallops 114

scurvy 12

shellfish, for fighting infection 29, 111

seeds 49, 56, 74, 75, 78, 80, 109, 110, 111, 114, 139, 155, 191, 192, 194, 196, 207, 210

skin 21–49, 101–2
    conditions 15, 25–6
    fighting infection 29
        foods for 29–30
    functions of 21–23
        and immune system 21–2
        and sensory organ 22–3

and temperature regulation 22
health, tips for 49
ingredients beneficial for 33–4
managing skin conditions 26–8
protecting key structures 30–1
    foods for 30–1
RECIPES FOR 33–48
regulating inflammation 27–8
    foods for 27–8
regulating oil production 28–9
structure of 23–5

spices 195–211

spinach 31, 109, 159–60, 215, 222

steak 160

stomach 52

subcutis 24–5

sugar 29, 49, 51, 54, 56, 57, 108, 111, 113, 114, 139, 159, 179, 185, 187, 188, 197, 200, 201, 219, 223, see also inulin
    refined 125, 151

sulphur 33, 78, 110, 202, 219, 220

sunflower seed 80–1

sweet potatoes 30, 34, 53, 57, 213, 223

synapse 154

synovial fluid 135, 136

synovial joints 134

tea, green 72

terminal, the 154

thyme 210

trace elements 12

tract, the 51–2

trout 137, 155

tumours 13, 104, 106, 176

turmeric, as an anti-inflammatory 81, 138, 142, 211, 221

urine 53
    infections 179

RECIPE INDEX

ACKNOWLEDGEMENTS

Clare, Natasha and Zoie – management gold dust. Thank you.

Tanya Murkett – with me from day one keeping me sane.

Dough and Heather, Ramsay and Candy, Mum and Dad.

And everyone who seeks the truth in this field and isn't led by fad fashion and folly.

This edition first published in Great Britain in 2017
by Orion Publishing Group Ltd
Carmelite House, 50 Victoria Embankment
London EC4Y 0DZ
An Hachette UK Company

1 3 5 7 9 10 8 6 4 2

Text © Dale Pinnock 2017
Design and layout © Orion Publishing Group Ltd 2017

A CIP catalogue record for this book
is available from the British Library.

ISBN: 9781409166368

Photography: Ria Osborne
Design: Clare Sivell
Props: Clare Sivell and Guiliana Casarotti
Home economist: Maud Eden
Illustrations on pages 197, 203 and 215: Rosie Webb

Printed and bound in Italy

This is an update of *Medicinal Cookery*,
first published by Constable & Robinson in 2011

www.orionbooks.co.uk